INSIGHT COMPACT GUIDE

COTS

Compact Guide: The Cotswolds is the ideal reference guide to this quintessentially English region. It tells you all you need to know about its attractions, from stone villages tucked into lush river valleys to Regency-style Cheltenham and the ancient city of Gloucester.

This is one of 130 Compact Guides, which combine the interests and enthusiasms of two of the world's best-known information providers: Insight Guides, whose titles have set the standard for visual travel guides since 1970, and Discovery Channel, the world's premier source of nonfiction television programming.

Star Attractions

An instant reference to some of the Cotswolds' most popular tourist attractions to help you on your way.

Folk Museum, Gloucester p19

Berkeley Castle p14

Gloucester Cathedral P20

National Waterways Museum p18

Owlpen Manor p26

Cirencester p34

Cheltenham p41

Sudeley Castle p45

Snowshill Manor p47

Chipping Campden p48

Winchcombe p45

The COTSWOLDS

Introduction

The Cotswolds' Rugged Harmony 5
Historical Highlights 10

Places

Route 1: Gloucester and the Vale of Berkeley **14**
Route 2: South Cotswolds **22**
Route 3: Stroud and the Mill Valleys **28**
Route 4: Cirencester and the Churn Valley **34**
Route 5: Cheltenham and the Cotswold Escarpment **41**
Route 6: Chipping Campden and
  the Gardens of the North Cotswolds **48**
Route 7: Around Stow-on-the-Wold **53**
Route 8: The Coln and Windrush Valleys **58**

Culture

Architecture and Gardens **65**
Festivals **67**

Leisure

Food and Drink **69**
Shopping **72**
Active Pursuits **73**

Practical Information

Getting There and Around **75**
Facts for the Visitor **76**
The Cotswolds for Children **77**
Accommodation **78**

Index **80**

The Cotswolds' Rugged Harmony

Opposite: typical Cotswold cottages

To countless thousands of people, the Cotswolds is the essence of England, a place where they would love to live – if not now, then at least when they retire. Laurie Lee, author of *Cider with Rosie* (1959), was lucky enough to be born near Slad, in 1914, where he spent most of his life. In 1995, two years before he died, he led a campaign to prevent the construction of a housing estate in his precious 'jungly, bird-crammed, insect-hopping valley'. Lee observed that the Cotswolds was 'easy to take for granted until you went away and discovered that the whole world was nothing like so special'.

Uley, tucked into the Cotswold hills

Here the hills are high and wild, but rarely bleak, and simple stone cottages combine with church, manor house and tithe barn to create a picture of timeless beauty. Stone here is plentiful, and massive lumps are pulled to the surface whenever the plough cuts the soil. It is this stone that gives the region its character, creating a harmonious landscape of fields bounded by drystone walls, churches with majestic towers, opulent town houses, stately homes and humble cottages with lichen-patched walls beneath steeply pitched roofs of limestone tile.

Sudeley Castle's gardens

Location and landscape

Stone also defines the boundaries of the Cotswolds. The region's creamy white oolitic limestone constitutes a distinctive geological feature. The Cotswold hills were formed from limestone created by the accumulation of shelly debris beneath the warm, shallow Midlands Sea that covered much of west-central England in ancient geological times. This thick compressed raft of calcium carbonate was later thrust up by tectonic pressure to create a tilted sheet running southwest to northeast.

To the north, west and south this sheet forms a cliff-like escarpment running from Mickleton, near Stratford-upon-Avon, southwards to Wotton-under-Edge, near Bath. Walkers can follow the length of the escarpment along the Cotswold Way, a long-distance footpath designated in 1970 and stretching 100 miles (160 km). In summer, with the mild southwesterly breezes behind you and sweeping views across the flat vale of the River Severn to the Malverns and to the Welsh mountains beyond, walking its length can be breathtaking. Its highest point, on Cleeve Hill, north of Cheltenham, rises to 1,040 ft (317 metres). The edge is littered with prehistoric hill-forts, burial mounds and the remains of ancient quarrying. The limestone grassland that tops these hills is rich in wildflowers, including rare orchids, which are festooned with butterflies.

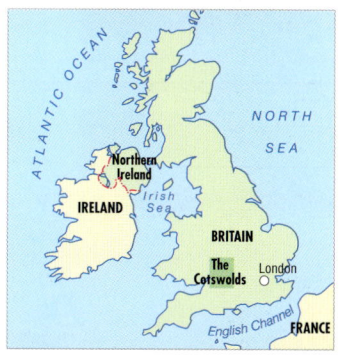

Inland from the escarpment, the dip slope of the Cotswolds descends by a steady gradient to meet the gravels of the upper Thames Valley. The change is marked by the increasing use of clay tiles for roofing and brick for walls. Towards Oxford, thatch takes over and the stone becomes honey coloured or even yellow, rather than the true Cotswold white or cream.

The Cotswolds have not always been regarded as the epitome of cosy rural Englishness. Shakespeare (in *Richard II*) described Gloucestershire as a county of 'high wild hills and rough uneven ways', while William Cobbett was equally scathing about the 'wild and wearisome hills'. In fact, your view of the Cotswolds depends entirely on where you are standing. Along the Fosse Way (A429), for example, or the Ermin Way (A417), it is tempting to agree that this is a soulless landscape of bleak and monotonous hills. Scanning the horizon across the stone-walled fields, there seem to be few signs of civilisation.

Ampney St Crucis

Turn off these main roads, however, and you will descend into wooded valleys with houses clustered around village greens, ancient churches surrounded by carved tea-caddy tombs and welcoming pubs. Most of the settlements in the Cotswolds are tucked into hidden hollows and valleys where they are invisible to anyone travelling on the high roads. In fact, one explanation of the name 'Cotswold' is that it means 'wooded hollows', from *wald*, the Saxon for wood, and *cote*, meaning a hollow, dugout or shelter (not surprisingly, there are rival explanations: *cot* could also mean a sheep enclosure, and *wolds* could also mean rolling hillsides).

Corner of a cottage garden

The prettiest Cotswold villages lie along the valleys of the Churn, Coln and Leach, the Eye, the Dikler and the Ampney Brook, the Windrush, the Frome and the many other brooks and streams that spring up in these hills to drain eventually into the Thames, Severn and Avon rivers. Many of these are misfit valleys (valleys that are very wide in proportion to the small streams that now flow through them), and were created by the meltwaters that flowed across the Cotswolds as the Midlands glaciers began to break up towards the end of the last Ice Age.

Once the glaciers were gone, the streams shrank to a fraction of their original size and settlements began to grow up along the sheltered valley sides. These provided natural terracing, fertile soils and shelter from the wind and snow of a Cotswolds' winter. In several places in the Cotswolds you can still gain a real feel for the enclosed nature of the landscape, the sense of inhabiting a secret magic world cut off from the rest of civilisation. Chedworth Roman villa *(see page 57)*, with its Italianate courtyards and bathhouses built into the shelter of the encircling hills, supplied by the pure waters of a crystal clear spring, is one place that evokes such an atmosphere. The same is true of magical Owlpen *(see page 26)*, set in its own owl-haunted valley near Uley, and of nearby Ozleworth, with its quirky Norman church set in the grounds of a Georgian country house, encircled by wooded hills *(see page 26)*. Equally special is Woodchester Park *(see page 26)*, a deep, secluded valley acquired by the National Trust and now open to the public after being virtually sealed off from the world since the late 19th century.

The Economy

The Romans introduced the distinctive long-woolled breed of sheep, known as the Cotswold Lions, on which the subsequent prosperity of the Cotswolds was based. Cotswold wool had already gained a Europe-wide reputation by the 11th century, and by the 14th century it was being exported to Flanders, Spain and Italy. The famous Merchant of Prato, Francesco di Marco Datini (whose letters and ledgers have given historians a fascinating insight into the life of a medieval textile merchant) claimed that the finest wool in the world came from the Cotswolds, and in particular from the area around Northleach.

Cornerstone of Cotswold history

Wool wealth paid for the churches of the Cotswolds, the majestic abbeys (many, such as Cirencester, erased from the face of the earth during the Dissolution) and the fine houses of the merchants in Cirencester, Chipping Campden, Painswick and Northleach. The Cotswolds continued to be a centre for textile production well into the early 20th century, with mills lining the banks of fast-flowing streams at Blockley, Chalford, Stroud and Nailsworth. These mills specialised in high-quality cloth, and at one time sold baize for soldiers' uniforms to both sides in the Napoleonic Wars. Even now, mills in the Chalford area produce cloth for tennis balls, billiard tables and the vestments of the pope.

Woolmarket, Cirencester

Taxation, combined with competition from South America, Australia and New Zealand, caused the Cotswold sheep industry to go into sharp decline in the 19th century, and the Cotswold Lion breed was only just rescued from extinction by a small group of enthusiasts who formed the Cotswold Sheep Society in 1892. Today you can see Cotswold Lions and other rare breeds at the Cotswold Farm Park *(see page 55)* and see wool being spun and woven at the Cotswold Woollen Weavers *(see page 61)*.

The Cotswolds remains an agricultural region, although much of the old sheep pasture has been ploughed up to grow crops. Cirencester is still home to the Royal Agricultural College, founded in 1845, Britain's premier institution for the teaching of agricultural science. It is a sign of the times, however, that the college has added Equine Studies to the syllabus, for, as a local joke has it, agriculture in this region is rapidly giving way to 'horsiculture'. This is partly because the Cotswolds has always been a region of large aristocratic estates, whose owners indulge in a hunting, shooting and fishing lifestyle. It is also because the glamourous and extremely profitable sports of polo and eventing have become entrenched in the area, bringing the rich and famous to the Cotswolds. Landowners have been quick to capitalise on the phenomenon, with events throughout the summer at Cirencester Park, Badminton and Gatcombe Park, home to the Princess Royal. Horsey types are everywhere in the Cotswolds, ranging from minor aristocrats to wealthy foreigners who rent Cotswold farmhouses for the season and fill the paddocks with polo ponies, before moving on to South Africa or South America for the winter. The novelist Jilly Cooper, who lives in Bisley *(see page 31)*, has brilliantly captured this side of life in the Cotswolds in her comic novels *Polo*, *Riders* and *Rivals*.

A mixed social gathering

Wild at heart

Conservation

Despite the ruggedness of its scenery, the beauty of the Cotswolds is very fragile. What looks like a timeless landscape is, in fact, changing all the time. In the Middle Ages, the Cotswolds consisted of unenclosed downland, providing uninterrupted grazing for vast flocks of sheep. In the 14th century, whole villages were depopulated to make way for sheep. A classic example is the deserted village of Upton, just west of Blockley *(see page 51)*, cleared in 1384 by the Bishops of Worcester, though the house platforms and streets remain clearly visible as earthworks.

Another great change occurred after 1750 when these great open sheepwalks began to be enclosed. It was at this time that many of the stone walls were built. Since 1945 the ploughing of pasture to create arable fields has changed the appearance of the Cotswolds yet again. Small fields have been merged to create larger ones by grubbing out hedges or removing walls.

Changes in farming methods have left many fine barns and farm buildings redundant. Some have been converted into dwellings with twee net curtains and mock Georgian front doors, introducing suburban values to the countryside. Where farmers have been refused permission to develop, they have left farm buildings to rot, often robbing them of masonry and stone roofing tiles before abandoning them to the elements.

Rare breeds at Cotswold Farm Park

A belated attempt has been made to hold back this tide of change. The Cotswolds is now officially an Area of Outstanding Natural Beauty, a designation that theoretically restricts development and provides government funds to encourage traditional low-intensity farming. Just about every town and village centre of note in the Cotswolds

River Windrush at Burford

is now a Conservation Area, which means development is kept to a minimum. Where new dwellings are permitted, they have to conform to strict design criteria, using recycled Cotswold stone, lime mortar and wood-framed windows. Permission is now rarely given to convert barns to dwellings, although they may be used for small-scale industrial activities.

With an area as distinctive as the Cotswolds, the local authorities tread a tightrope. On the one hand they must maintain the life of the area and provide for employment and housing; on the other they have to try and preserve the essential character that attracts tourism and makes the Cotswolds such a desirable place to live. This has been achieved by allowing towns such as Cirencester and Stroud to develop while conserving others, such as Northleach, Stow-on-the-Wold and Chipping Campden.

Making the most of the Cotswolds

The Cotswolds is a very private region, yet there are seasonal opportunities to go behind the high walls of the aristocratic estates. More private gardens are open in Gloucestershire during the spring and summer than in any other county in England. Visiting them also provides the opportunity to admire some outstanding architecture, not to mention indulging in the thoroughly English habit of consuming homemade cakes and cups of tea. To find out more, consult the 'Yellow Book' (*Gardens of England and Wales Open for Charity*, available in most bookshops), and get hold of a guide to gardens open under the Red Cross scheme (available at tourist information centres).

Wildlife is particularly abundant in Gloucestershire. The county has more species and more different habitats than any other in England. For a guide to what to see where, consult the *Reserve Handbook*, published by the Gloucestershire Wildlife Trust (tel: 01452 383333).

Morris man, Lechlade

Snowshill Manor

Historical Highlights

3000–2000 BC Woodland clearance marks the beginnings of settlement and agriculture. Paleolithic (Old Stone Age) sites have been excavated on the Thames gravels at Bourton-on-the-Water and Lechlade. Neolithic (New Stone Age) settlements on Leckhampton Hill and on Crickley Hill, on the escarpment above Cheltenham, where archaeologists have found flint arrow heads, scrapers and knives. The most visible relics of this era are the long barrows – burial mounds covering chambered tombs of stone. Hetty Peglar's Tump above Uley, and Belas Knap near Winchcombe are outstanding examples.

1,800 BC Hundreds of round barrows (burial mounds) show the scale of Bronze Age settlement.

1,000 BC Iron Age (Celtic) migrants colonise the Cotswolds on a massive scale. Over the next millennium they develop a society every bit as sophisticated as that of the early medieval period. The success of the Iron Age peoples of southern Britain in metalworking, grain, wool and dye production and animal husbandry was a reason for the Roman invasion. Fine examples of Iron Age hillforts include, from south to north, Little Sodbury, Uley Bury, Haresfield Beacon, Painswick Beacon, Crickley Hill, Leckhampton Hill and Cleeve Hill. The Birdlip Mirror, in Gloucester City Museum, reveals the sophistication of Celtic art of this era, and coinage, currency bars and pottery in the Corinium Museum, Cirencester, shows a well developed economy.

AD 43 After the Romans invade England, the Celtic Dobuni tribe (whose capital was at Bagendon) at first resist, throwing up defences on Minchinhampton Common (The Bulwarks), but later agree to a truce and become administrators for the new rulers, based in the newly founded Corinium Dobunorum (Cirencester). The basic road grid for Gloucestershire was established (and remains in use) with Cirencester at the hub. Gloucester (Glevum) is founded as a temporary encampment for the XXth legion, which moves to permanent headquarters at Caerleon, in Wales.

200 By now Corinium is the second largest town in Roman Britain, its town walls enclosing 240 acres (97 hectares). The vigour of the local economy is indicated by the scale of town houses (finds are in the Corinium Museum) and by the wealthy villas and farmsteads in the surrounding countryside. An accomplished school of mosaic-makers based in Cirencester supplied wealthy locals with very fine Roman mosaic floors.

5th century AD The sudden breakdown in administrative authority in the region is illustrated by the fortification of the Roman amphitheatre at Cirencester and the fact that the previously clean streets and ditches around the forum begin to accumulate debris, including human corpses. Villas continue to function as farmsteads, and finds in Cirencester museum marked with symbols suggest the adoption of Christianity by the elite.

577 The *Anglo-Saxon Chronicle* records that the native Britons were defeated by invading Saxons at the Battle of Dyrham (on the escarpment south of Chipping Sodbury), that three British kings were killed and that subsequently the walled towns of Gloucester, Cirencester and Bath were captured. The Cotswolds now becomes part of the Anglo-Saxon Kingdom of Wessex.

10th–11th century Christianity spreads slowly amongst the Anglo-Saxon kingdoms. By the 10th century there are several Saxon monastic institutions in the region, including St Oswald's Priory in Gloucester, built by Aethelflaed, Queen of Mercia and daughter of Alfred the Great. Saxon churches at Coln St Dennis and Middle Duntisbourne, and carvings in churches in Bibury and Daglingworth, indicate the quality of architecture on the eve of the Norman conquest.

1066 After William the Conqueror's coronation, the Normans embark on a programme of castle and church building. Gloucester Cathedral is rebuilt, and is one of the few cathedrals in England to survive substantially in its Norman form. Parish churches survive with fine Romanesque lead fonts and rare carvings.

1085 While holding court in Gloucester, William the Conqueror orders the *Domesday Book* to be compiled.

1246 Hailes Abbey is founded by King John's son, the Earl of Cornwall.

1327 Edward II is brutally murdered at Berkeley Castle. His shrine at Gloucester Cathedral attracts so many pilgrims that their donations enable the east end of the church to be rebuilt.

1535–40 The Dissolution of the English and Welsh monasteries under Thomas Cromwell results in the break up of the fabulously wealthy monastic estates of Cirencester, Winchcombe, Hailes and Gloucester. The buildings are demolished for building stone and the lands are given or sold to friends of the monarch.

1536 Cotswolds-born William Tyndale, the first person to translate the Bible into English, is burned at the stake for heresy.

1547 Catherine Parr remarries six weeks after the death of Henry VIII and moves to Sudeley Castle. She dies the following year after giving birth, and is buried in the castle chapel.

1612 With royal support, Robert Dover institutes the Cotswold Olympicks at Chipping Campden to encourage the pursuit of manly sports.

1642 Lord Chandos makes Sudeley Castle a Royalist stronghold at the start of the Civil War. Parliamentary towns Cirencester and Gloucester are unsuccessfully besieged by Royalists.

1643 The Civil War siege of Painswick.

1644 Sudeley Castle falls to the Royalists and is partially demolished to make it unusable as a fortress.

1646 The final battle of the Civil War is fought at Stow-on-the-Wold.

1714–18 Cirencester Park, a pioneering example of the English landscape school, is laid out by the First Earl Bathurst and his friend, the poet Alexander Pope.

1716 Discovery of the mineral springs that will result in the massive growth of Cheltenham, turning it into the Cotswolds' largest town.

1788 George II visits Cheltenham Spa, setting the seal on its fashionable reputation.

1789 Opening of the Thames and Severn Canal linking Bristol with London.

1796 Edward Jenner invents the world's first vaccine by inoculating a boy against smallpox at his home in Berkeley.

1829 The first trees are planted on the estate that will eventually be known as Westonbirt Arboretum, in Gloucestershire.

1871 William Morris first rents Kelmscott manor as his country home.

1874 Gustav Holst is born in Cheltenham of Swedish parents.

1892 The Cotswold Sheep Society is formed to save the now endangered breed, introduced by the Romans, on which the Cotswolds' medieval prosperity was largely based.

1902 C.R. Ashbee forms the Guild of Handicrafts in Chipping Campden, espousing the utopian ideals of William Morris.

1907 Laurence Johnstone begins making the garden at Hidcote.

1939–45 Several major air bases are used by the British and US air forces as bases for bombing raids against Germany and occupied Europe – several, including South Cerney, Brize Norton and Fairford, are still in use as NATO air bases.

1946 Sir Peter Scott founds the Slimbridge Wildfowl and Wetlands Trust.

1959 Laurie Lee's novel *Cider with Rosie,* celebrating his Cotswold childhood, is published.

1980s Prince Charles develops his gardening and organic farming ideas from his home at Highgrove, just outside Tetbury.

1996 The Cotswolds is designated as an Area of Outstanding Natural Beauty.

2000 *Harry Potter and the Sorcerer's Stone*, an adaption of J.K. Rowling's children's bestseller, is filmed at Gloucester Cathedral.

2002 The Waterways Trust announces that the Thames and Severn Canal will be cleaned and reopened, with funding from The Lottery, once again creating a navigable link between these two great rivers.

Gloucester's Norman Cathedral

Route 1

Gloucester and the Vale of Berkeley

Berkeley – Sharpness – Slimbridge Wildfowl & Wetlands Trust – Frampton on Severn – Hardwicke Court – Gloucester *See map page 16*

Lying between the River Severn to the west and the steep Cotswold escarpment to the east, the Vale of Berkeley is an area of rich pasture and small dairy farms. Red-brown Gloucester cows (now a rare breed which can be seen at the Cotswold Farm Park – *see page 55*) were once raised here to produce creamy Single and Double Gloucester cheeses. In the 18th century, a local doctor, Edward Jenner, noted in the course of his work that the local milkmaids who contracted cowpox, a minor disease, became immune to smallpox, a disease that killed thousands of children every year and left thousands more blinded or scarred for life. In 1796 Jenner vaccinated a local boy with cowpox, and thus invented the science of immunology, as well as the practice of vaccination.

The remarkable story of Jenner's research and the development of the world's first vaccine is told through films and displays at the ★★ **Jenner Museum** in Berkeley (tel: 01453 810631; open Apr–Sept, Tues–Sat and bank holidays 12.30–5.30pm, Sun 1–5.30pm; Oct, Sun only). Among the exhibits are 18th-century cartoons satirising Jenner and his patients as bovine country buffoons. Jenner does not enjoy the regard that you might expect in England, a fact illustrated by the fact that this fascinating museum was paid for by a Japanese philanthropist.

Jenner Museum

★★★ **Berkeley Castle** is the site where Edward II was brutally murdered in 1327. Despite being a party to regicide, the Lords Berkeley managed to hang on to their magnificent feudal castle, which has passed through 24 generations of the same family from 1153 to the present day (tel: 01453 810332; open Apr and May, Tues–Sun 2–5pm; Jun–Sept, Tues–Sat 11am–5pm, Sun 2–5pm; also Mon in Jul, Aug and bank holidays; Oct, Sun 2–4pm). The castle looks the part, with its massive Norman keep (built 1067), the cell where Edward spent his last days and the Great Hall, where the English barons held their last meeting before riding to Runnymede to force King John to set his seal to the Magna Carta.

Berkeley Castle

A fine terraced garden surrounds the castle and there is a ★ **Butterfly Farm** in the grounds (run as a separate enterprise but open similar hours). In the ★ **church** alongside the castle, fine alabaster effigies commemorate the Berkeleys and their wives, but it is worth seeking out the two table tombs of lesser mortals in the churchyard. One marks the burial place of England's last court jester (died 1728), whose grave bears an epitaph penned by Jonathan Swift, while the other has an equally witty engraving summing up the life of Thomas Pearce, a local watchmaker (died 1665).

Berkeley attraction

Four miles (6 km) north of Berkeley is the Severnside port town of ★ **Sharpness**, with its busy container terminal. The town was founded in 1794 when the Gloucester and Sharpness Canal was dug so that ships could sail directly to Gloucester without having to navigate the difficult tidal waters of the River Severn. The canal remains in use, and is capable of taking ships as large as 1,000 tonnes. Sharpness is also the centre of the local elver fishing industry. Elvers are young eels that are carried by the Gulf Stream from the Sargasso Sea, where they hatch, to the rivers of northern Europe, where they grow to adults, before returning to the Sargasso to breed and die. The elvers are netted along these banks and held in storage tanks at Sharpness for export to Holland and Germany, where smoked eel is a prized delicacy.

Industrial Sharpness

You will encounter the canal again if you visit Slimbridge, for the road to the ★★★ **Wildfowl and Wetlands Centre** passes over one of several bridges that swing aside to let ships and pleasure boats through. The Centre (tel: 01453 890333; open daily summer, 9.30am–5pm; winter, 9.30am–4pm) was founded in 1946 by the artist and naturalist Sir Peter Scott on a marshy site beside the Severn that naturally attracts large numbers of wild birds. These can be seen from hides dotted discreetly around the margins of the site, while the ponds around the reserve are home to a great array of wildfowl from all over the world. From the entrance the route passes through a visitor centre with displays explaining the ecology of wetland habitats around the world. If watching and feeding birds is

Along the canal, Slimbridge

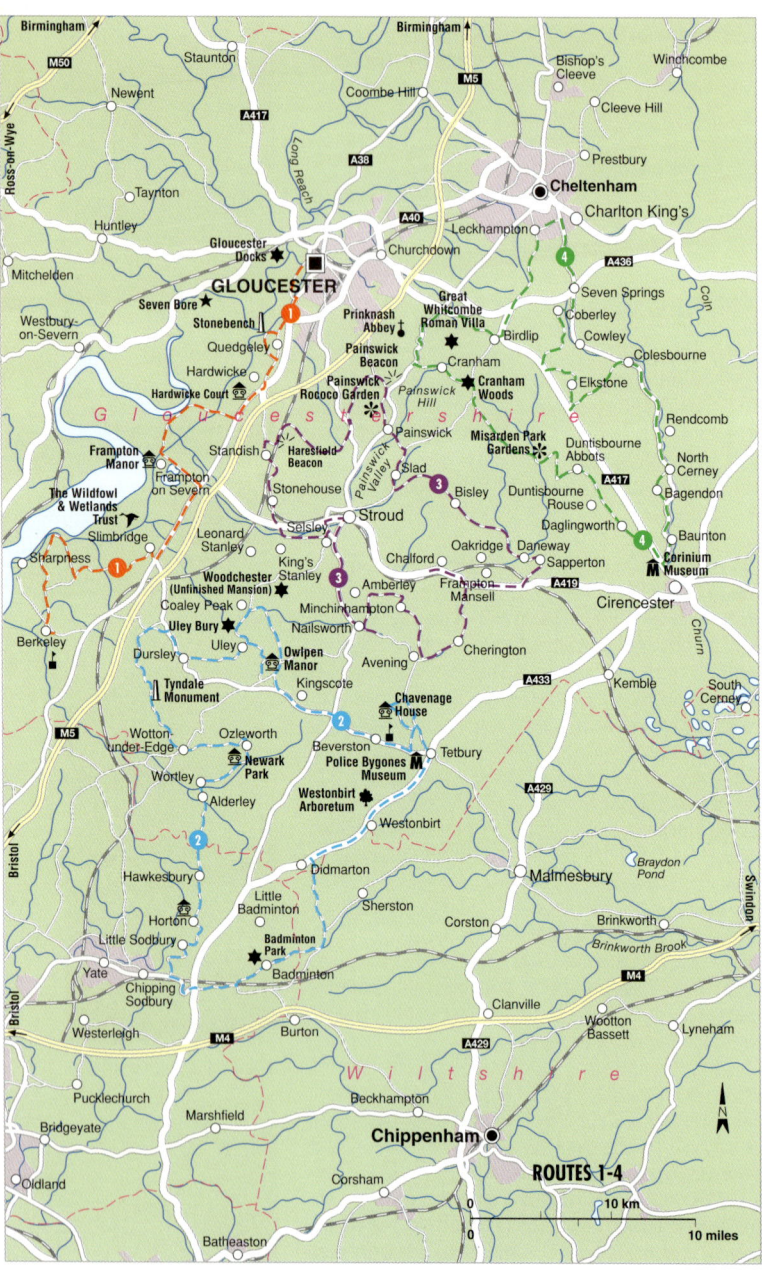

too sedentary an activity for your children, you could take them instead to **Berkeley Heath Farm**, better known as **Cattle Country** (tel: 01453 810510; open school holidays and every Sunday 10am–5pm) for its farm trail (complete with roaming bison), its rodeo shows, birds of prey demonstrations and a big adventure playground with zip wires and 'Wall of Death' slides.

Before leaving the Slimbridge area, take the chance to visit the village ★ church, an unusually complete example of the 13th-century Early English style, with fine foliated capitals and an unusual lead font of 1664.

Four miles (6 km) north on the A38, turn left for ★ **Frampton on Severn**, set around England's largest village green. Formerly a marsh and still dotted with bird-filled ponds, the green was created in the early 18th century when Richard Clutterbuck, a wealthy official at the Bristol Customs House, built **Frampton Court**, the huge Palladian building visible behind the high wall to the east of the green (the Gothic revival-style Orangery of 1743 is more easily seen). In the mid-1980s, 300 19th-century watercolours of local wildflowers were found in the Court's attics and were published as the *Frampton Flora*. Today the owner gives guided tours of this fine historic house and you can enjoy bed-and-breakfast in the Tapestry Room with views over the grounds and lake (tel: 01452 740267 to book tours and accommodation).

On the opposite side of the green are charming timber houses, including ★★ **Frampton Manor** (also known as Manor Farmhouse), a fine mid-15th century building with a delightful garden (tel: 01452 740698; house and gardens open by appointment all year). The manor is reputed to be the birthplace of 'Fair Rosamund' Clifford (died 1176), the celebrated mistress of Henry II. Just beyond the manor is the ★ **church**, which has a notable late 12th-century Romanesque lead font depicting the Evangelists.

At ★ Arlingham, set in a loop of the River Severn 4 miles (6 km) west, ★ **St Augustine's Farm** allows children to make friends with rabbits, goats, hens and calves (tel: 01452 740277; open Easter–Sept, Tues–Sun and bank holidays 11am–5pm). One mile (1.6 km) west is the site of an important prehistoric river crossing, used by Welsh cattle drovers until quite recent times. Now twitchers come here to watch wading birds.

If you want to watch the **Severn Bore**, you need to follow the back lanes that thread this part of the Vale to Framilode, Epney, Elmore or Stonebench. For further information, visit the website at www.severn-bore.co.uk The bore is a large wave (one of the biggest river waves in the world, with a height of 25ft/7.5m in spring, and a top speed of 15 knots/27kph) – fast enough to attract surfers in search of novelty and challenge), which travels up the estuary

On the village green, Frampton

River Severn

Mooring at the National Waterways Museum

Gloucester city centre

Narrowboats

'Queen Boadicea'

from Avonmouth to Gloucester. Spring brings the most impressive waves, but the bore can be seen at regular intervals throughout the year.

Another spot to seek out as you head for Gloucester is ★ **Hardwicke Court**, which lies on the west side of the A38 south of the village of Hardwicke itself (tel: 01452 720212; open Easter Mon–30 Sep, Mon 2–4pm or by prior appointment). The building is not signposted so you will need to keep your eyes open. Built in 1818 by Sir Robert Smirke (architect of the British Museum), the house is of great interest architecturally and includes several fine family portraits.

★★★ **Gloucester** is not one of England's most beautiful cities, though it is a place of enormous historical interest. The city was founded by the Romans shortly after the invasion of AD 43 as a temporary encampment for the XXth Legion, which moved to permanent headquarters at Caerleon, in Wales, in AD 75. Gloucester then became a *colonia* (a settlement for retired army veterans), and from this point it grew to become a major Saxon town, with a mint and a monastery. William the Conqueror held court here and it was here, in 1085, that he ordered the *Domesday Book* to be compiled. By the 16th century, Gloucester had also become a major port, shipping corn, timber, slate, metals, wines and spirits.

Recently the docklands area has been restored, and there are several attractions set in 19th-century warehouses around the dock basin. The excellent, child-friendly ★★★ **National Waterways Museum** ❶ has hands-on activities, interactive displays and video presentations, not to mention narrowboats and a steam dredger to explore (tel: 01452 318054; open daily 10am–5pm). The museum tells the story of England's commercial waterways, from the canal-building mania of the late 18th century to their decline in the 20th century, brought about by the combined competition of road and rail transport. Exhibits cover canal construction, wildlife, cargoes and life on a narrowboat.

Moored beside the museum is ★ *Queen Boadicea II* (built as a Thames passenger ship in 1936). You can board and take a 45-minute cruise through Gloucester Port and along the Gloucester and Sharpness Canal; a commentary is included in the price of a ticket (tel: 01452 318054 for details and advance bookings; there are also longer cruises to Tewkesbury in summer).

Another of the dockland museums concerns the altogether more sober subject of warfare. The ★ **Soldiers of Gloucestershire Museum** ❷ (tel: 01452 522682; open 10–5pm Sep–June Tues–Sun and bank holidays; Jul–Aug, daily 10am–5pm) covers the history of the Gloucestershire regiments from the late 17th century, with a reconstruction of a World War I trench and sections on women at war and Northern Ireland.

Almost opposite this museum are the red-brick walls of Gloucester Gaol, still a fully operational prison. Beyond the gaol, following signs to the centre, you should end up in Westgate Street – if not, you are unlikely to get lost, because the centre retains its Roman grid layout, with four main streets: Westgate, Northgate, Eastgate and Southgate Street. At the end of Westgate Street furthest from the centre is the ★★ **Gloucester Folk Museum** ❸ (tel: 01452 396467; open Mon–Sat 10am–5pm; Jul–Sept, open Sun also, 10am–4pm). The museum occupies a fine timber-framed merchant's house built around 1500, now packed with a miscellaneous collection of objects from working model railways and a stuffed Gloucester Old Spot pig to displays showing traditional methods of fishing for salmon and elvers in the River Severn. The Civil War Siege of Gloucester (1643) and the history of the port are both covered in detail, and the museum has a good programme of activites for children at weekends and during school holidays.

On the opposite side of Westgate Street, narrow lanes lead through to the cathedral close. One of these lanes – College

Sign of a time

An eclectic collection

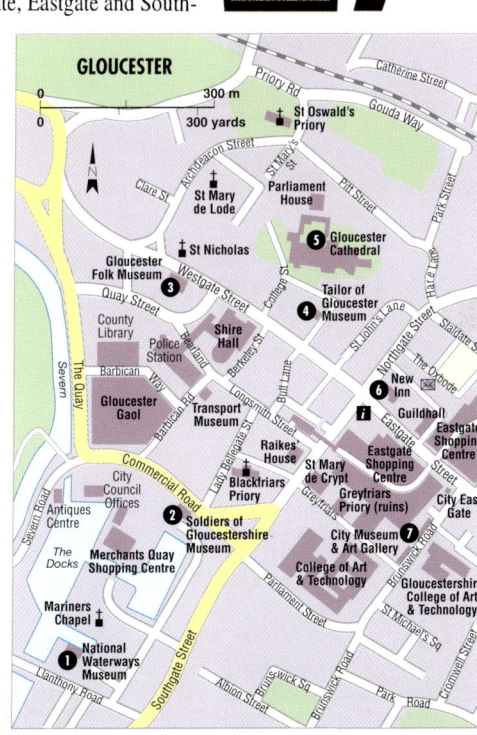

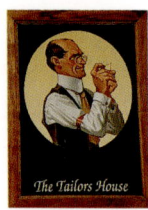

Tailor of Gloucester Museum

Gloucester Cathedral

Robert Duke of Normandy

Court – is lined with timber houses, including the Beatrix Potter Gift Shop and ★ **Tailor of Gloucester Museum** ❹ (tel: 01452 422856; open Apr–Oct, daily 10am–5pm; Nov–Mar: daily 10am–4pm, closed Sun and bank holidays). The famous story about the Tailor of Gloucester by Beatrix Potter (1899–1943) was based on real people and events. The tailor was one John Prichard who had been commissioned to make a waistcoat for the Mayor of Gloucester. Having cut out the parts, he left his shop for the weekend and returned to find the waistcoat complete, with the exception of one buttonhole. A note pinned to the garment explained 'No more twist'. From that time on, Prichard advertised his services with a sign saying: 'Come to Prichard where the waistcoats are made at night by fairies.' Years later, two of his assistants revealed that they had let themselves into the workshop and sewn up the waistcoat for a joke.

This shop in College Court is not the original tailor's premises, but it is the one that Beatrix Potter used as the inspiration for the watercolours she painted to accompany her tale. The museum contains first editions of Potter's books, a replica of the waistcoat in her tale (embroidered by members of the Women's Institute) and working models based on illustrations from Potter's works.

From the passageway of College Court, you emerge on College Green, with a fine view of ★★★ **Gloucester Cathedral** ❺ (tel 01452 528095; open summer, daily 8am–6pm; winter, daily 8am–5pm, though parts of the church may be closed off for services). This fine Norman church is relatively small by cathedral standards. The nave, with its massive columns, dates from Abbot Serlo's building campaign which began in 1089 and ended in 1121. The other great building period began in the 14th century, after Edward II, murdered at Berkeley Castle in 1327, was brought to this church for burial. The combined income from the pilgrims who flocked to the late king's tomb, and the funds donated by successive English monarchs in expiation of the regicide, funded the reconstruction of the cathedral's choir and transepts.

The marvellous east window, which fills the entire east wall of the nave, dates from this period, as do the choir stalls with their misericords (one of which is carved with an early representation of the game of football). Two tombs in the choir are not to be missed: the very fine wooden effigy of Robert Duke of Normandy, William the Conqueror's eldest son, depicted in crusading armour on the southern side, and the shrine of Edward II himself, on the northern side, lying with his head supported by cherubs. Off the north aisle is Gloucester's chief claim to architectural innovation. The ceiling of the cloister is beautifully decorated with fan vaulting – invented in

Gloucester and later used in King's College Chapel and the Chapel Royal at Windsor. While these might be of interest to adults, children will be far more enthralled by the fact that the cloister was used as one of the locations for filming *Harry Potter and the Philosopher's Stone* (2001). See if your children can spot the difference between the stone vaulted cloister and the corridors of Hogwarts School.

The 'Hogwarts' cloister

From the cathedral, follow Westgate Street into the centre of town where the two principal axes meet at **the Cross**. The original medieval cross has long gone, but there are several notable buildings nearby. At the crossroads itself is the tower of St Michael's church, now serving as the tourist information centre. A short way up Northgate Street is **New Inn** ❻, a rare surviving example of an enclosed courtyard inn, with tiers of open galleries. The Inn was built in 1457 to accommodate pilgrims visiting Edward II's tomb. A short way up Southgate Street is a 1904 shopfront belonging to Baker's the jewellers. This is of interest primarily because of its fine figure clock. The elaborate timepiece features Father Time, John Bull, a kilted Scotsman and women in Irish and Welsh national dress, all holding the bells that strike the hours. Two doors up is the flamboyant Jacobean timber facade of the townhouse of the Lords Berkeley (1650).

Baker's the jewellers

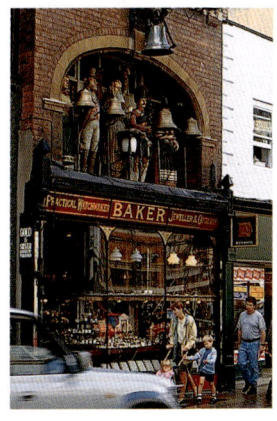

In Eastgate Street, remains of the Roman East Gate survive below modern street level and can be viewed through a glass superstructure let into the pavement. Just beyond, on the right, Brunswick Road leads to the ★★ **City Museum and Art Gallery** ❼, where the various strands of Gloucester's history are drawn together (tel: 01452 396131; open Mon–Sat, 10am–5pm; Jul–Sept, open Sun additionally, 10am–4pm). There are excellent displays of dinosaurs and fossils, local flora and fauna, furniture, silver, porcelain, clocks and paintings, but the star exhibits are nearly all archaeological. They include the outstanding 10th-century Saxon sculpture displayed in the museum foyer, found during recent excavation of St Oswald's Priory, built by Aethelflaed, Queen of Mercia and daughter of Alfred the Great, and the intricately carved bone and ivory backgammon set, dating from the 1070s. Two exhibits in bronze were made more than 1,500 years apart: the Birdlip mirror (so-called because it was excavated from the grave of a 35-year-old woman on Birdlip Hill) is an outstanding example of pre-Roman Celtic design, with an intricate geometric pattern filled with enamel, while the closing ring made for St Nicholas church, Westgate, in 1300 is an extraordinary example of medieval metalworking, cast in the form of a man poking his tongue out and wearing a hood that takes the form of a horned and winged demon.

Route 2

South Cotswolds

Tetbury – Westonbirt – Didmarton – Badminton – Little Sodbury – Horton – Hawkesbury – Alderley – Ozleworth – Newark Park – Wotton-under-Edge – North Nibley – Uley – Owlpen Valley – Woodchester Park – Beverston Castle *See map page 16*

Tetbury

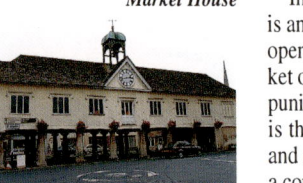

Market House

Police Bygones Museum

★★ **Tetbury** was a quiet little backwater until Prince Charles moved to Highgrove, on the southern outskirts of the town, delighting local estate agents who now describe property in the area as 'situated in Royal Gloucestershire'. Many of the 17th/18th-century townhouses lining Long Street (Tetbury's main street) are now the premises of antique dealers, so if you are interested in seeing what these houses look like inside you can always feign an interest in buying an old oak dresser or Georgian corner cupboard. No excuse is needed to gain admission to the ★ **Police Bygones Museum** (63 Long Street, tel: 01666 504670, open Mar–Nov, Mon–Fri 10am–3pm) which shares a building with the tourist information centre. It displays relics of Cotswold law enforcement in the old cells of the former police station.

In the centre of the town, the Market House of 1655 is an elegant structure on stone pillars with space for an open market below and a covered market upstairs (market on Wed/Fri). Off to the left is Gumstool Hill, with its punishingly steep incline. Every Spring Bank Holiday this is the site of a woolsack race when contestants run up and down the hill carrying a 66-lb (30-kg) bale of wool, a contest which probably started as a trial of strength between young farmers, designed to impress the local girls.

Tetbury's glory is its wonderfully theatrical ★★ **church**, a very rare example of Georgian Gothic, built in 1781 and with nearly all its furnishings intact. What has changed (as you can see from old photographs hung on the nave wall) is the position of the pulpit. If you stand where the pulpit once stood, you really do feel like an actor standing centre stage, with tiers of seating rising all around you.

Heading south out of Tetbury on the A433 Bath Road, you will pass Prince Charles's home, Highgrove House, on the right after 2 miles (3 km), though it is hidden behind high walls. Opposite is **Doughton Manor**, an almost untouched 17th-century house with a fine barn which probably dates from medieval times.

Two miles (3 km) on is ★★★ **Westonbirt Arboretum** (tel: 01666 880220; open daily 10am–8pm or sunset if earlier). This glorious estate was created in 1829 by the 21-year-old Robert Holford, who planted many of the fine trees that give the arboretum its structure. Interplanted among the trees are avenues of camellias, azaleas, rhododendrons, magnolias, cherries and maples. These beautiful shrubs and trees bring thousands to Westonbirt during May and October for the spring and autumn colours. For the rest of the year Westonbirt is relatively quiet, though there is always something to see.

Westonbirt Arboretum

The arboretum represents only a small part of Robert Holford's estate. He also owned the village of ★ **Westonbirt** on the opposite side of the road, and all the land surrounding his huge mansion (now the Westonbirt School for Girls). The Italianate terraced gardens of Westonbirt are occasionally open under the National Gardens Scheme. Failing that, go to the churchyard for a good view of the gardens and the school, a flamboyant French-style neo-baroque building designed in 1863 by Vulliamy. Holford has a magnificent mock-medieval tomb in the church. The former squire of Westonbirt and MP for East Gloucestershire is portrayed in effigy wearing a skull cap and ermine-trimmed gown with a greyhound at his feet.

Westonbirt School for Girls

The next village south is ★ **Didmarton**, which has a heartening story for those who love old churches. Here the 19th-century parishioners wanted a modern church, but they built a new one on a greenfield site further up the Bath road, leaving the characterful medieval church unchanged. Today's parishioners have brought the old church back into use, returning all the furnishings, including the brass chandeliers and the altar table, that had been removed to the Victorian church. Didmarton's church is a treat. It is set peacefully opposite a spring known locally as St Lawrence's Holy Well, and stands adjacent to the 17th-century manor and tithe barn.

Didmarton's medieval church

Continuing along the Bath road, you will pass the Worcester Lodge entrance to **Badminton Park** on the left,

Great Badminton

an imposing domed Palladian structure designed by William Kent around 1746. This is all you will see of Badminton Park unless you happen to be here for the horse trials in May or when the fine gardens are open under the National Gardens Scheme in June. You can drive through the estate, however, taking the next left to **Little Badminton**, where the church stands on one side of a big green with a dovecote and several pretty thatched farm cottages, and on to **Great Badminton**, with its imposing 18th-century estate houses. These are not low cottages, but terraces of nobly proportioned houses, with pediments carrying the Beaufort coat of arms, rendered and limewashed in pink and caramel. As proof of the architectural variety of the Georgian era, look out, as you drive through Great Badminton towards Acton Turville, for the *cottages ornés* with deeply overhanging thatched roofs supported on rustic posts, and for farm buildings disguised as follies with Georgian Gothic windows and battlements.

From Acton Turville, head west towards Chipping Sodbury, through Old Sodbury and then right for Little Sodbury. Here we are right on the southern edge of the Cotswolds proper, although the limestone breaks out again further south around Bath and Bristol (see *Insight Compact Guide: Bath* for a detailed guide to this region). Just before you reach Little Sodbury, you can pull off the road and walk up a broad footpath to ★ **Little Sodbury hillfort**, built in the Iron Age with massive double ramparts and commanding views that stretch westwards over the Forest of Dean and Wales. The church here is far less imposing, a humble structure built in 1659 from masonry taken from the demolished Little Chapel, behind Little Sodbury manor, where William Tyndale (*see page 25*) preached in the 1520s. It was here that he was first inspired with the idea of translating the Bible into English.

Little Sodbury hillfort

At ★ **Horton**, two miles (3.2 km) north, the Court belongs to the National Trust, though only the 12th-century hall is open to the public (tel: 01249 730141; open Apr–Oct, Wed and Sat 2–6pm). If you are here when it is closed you can get a good view from the churchyard. The fine ★ **church** porch has capitals carved with a lion and a dragon, and men playing flute and bagpipes. The light and airy church has a handsome Jacobean pulpit on an older stone base.

Horton Court

Driving on northwards to Hawkesbury, the road passes along the Cotswold escarpment through unploughed sheep pasture which bears the marks of ancient agriculture in the form of ditches, banks and terraces. **Hawkesbury** itself is worth a visit just for the fine 15th-century ★ **church** (often locked) with its monument to Lord Liverpool (died 1828), prime minister at the time of the Battle of Waterloo. ★ **Alderley church** is a pretty Georgian Gothic structure, now serving as the chapel to the adjacent Rosehill school; in the churchyard is the grave of the celebrated botanical artist Marianne North (1830–90), whose works are displayed at Kew Botanical Gardens.

Beyond Alderley, a right turn leads into one of several isolated and forgotten valleys that make exploring the Cotswolds such an adventure. The road runs along Ozleworth Bottom to the gates of Ozleworth Park. A public footpath runs through the park grounds to ★★ **Ozleworth church**, a curious Romanesque structure with a hexagonal central tower. The circular churchyard is surrounded by a drystone wall marking the boundary of an even older burial ground, thought to date from the 5th–6th century. Ozleworth village is no more, and the only other building in this wooded combe is Ozleworth House, an early 18th-century mansion with a contemporary bathhouse in the grounds (occasionally open in summer).

Ozleworth Church detail

Continue uphill from Ozleworth and left to ★★ **Newark Park** (National Trust, tel: 01453 842644; open April and May, Wed and Thurs 11am–5pm; June–Sept, Wed, Thur, Sat and Sun, 11am–5pm). Newark (a contraction of 'New Work') was built as a hunting lodge by Sir Nicholas Poyntz in 1540 using timber and masonry from the demolished Kingswood Abbey, near Wotton-under-Edge. James Wyatt remodelled the house in 1790, giving it neo-Gothic external details and Adam-style interiors.

Newark Park

From these lonely valleys it is quite a contrast to return to the bustle of ★ **Wotton-under-Edge**, a former mill town with a small heritage centre in the former fire station at The Chipping (tel: 01453-521541, open Tue–Fri, 10am––1pm and 2pm–5pm; Sat, mornings only). North of Wotton, along the B4060, the escarpment becomes increasingly steep as you approach North Nibley, where there is a car park at the entrance to the village and a footpath up through beech woods to the ★★ **Tyndale Monument** on Nibley Knoll. William Tyndale was burned at the stake in 1536 for heresy – his crime was to translate the Bible into English, a revolutionary act condemned by a Church fearful that its authority would be undermined if people could read and interpret the Bible for themselves. Tyndale's labours were not entirely in vain, for large parts of his translation were incorporated into the Authorised King James Version of 1611. The Tyndale Monument takes the form of a tower, 111 ft (34 metres) high, which can be climbed for sweeping views. It was built in 1866 in the belief that Tyndale was born in North Nibley, but it is now thought he may have been born in the Welsh Marches.

Wotton-under-Edge clock

Tyndale Monument

Stinchcombe Hill, 2 miles (3.2 km) further north, is another fine viewpoint, the last stretch of greenery before

Views of Owlpen Manor

you reach the former textile towns of Cam and Dursley. In Dursley, just past the market house and town hall of 1738 with its statue of Queen Anne, take the B4066 east to ★ **Uley**. This former mill village was once famous for its blue cloth and for the militancy of its weavers, who formed illegal and secret trade societies (the forerunners of trade unions) to maintain the value of their wages. Lower down in the village are rows of weavers cottages, whilst around the green are the houses of the mill owners and merchants. The church, though rebuilt in 1857 under the influence of the evangelical Oxford Movement, has some fine tea-caddy tombs in its churchyard.

From Uley's green, a narrow road heads east into the hidden **Owlpen Valley**, with its beautiful 15th-century ★★ **Manor** (tel: 01453 860261; open Apr 1–Sept 30, Tue–Sun and bank holidays 2–5pm). Dating back to at least 1464, the manor escaped improvements and stood empty between 1850–1926, when the art-and-crafts architect Norman Jewson restored it with a lively appreciation for its beauty, antiquity and setting. Highlights include the Cotswold arts-and-crafts movement furniture, and the 17th-century painted cloth wall hangings in the bedroom. The early 18th-century gardens were described by Vita Sackville-West as 'a dream…amongst dark secret rooms of yew, hiding in the valley'. There are lovely walks through the wooded valley to the other buildings of the estate (now converted to holiday accommodation), such as the 18th-century grist mill. Behind the manor is the small but ornate Victorian church, decorated with mosaics, stained glass and encaustic tiles.

Back in Uley the steep road out of the village passes several important prehistoric monuments. First comes **Uley Bury Iron Age hillfort**, one of the most spectacularly sited in the Cotswolds, with extensive views from the summit. Less than a mile north is ★ **Hetty Pegler's Tump**, one of the best-preserved neolithic long barrows in the Cotswolds. Named after Hetty Pegler, who owned the land in the 17th century, the tump was built around 3000 BC, and deliberately sited on this prominent hilltop so as to be visible from afar.

Hetty Pegler's Tump

There is another similar barrow, with explanatory boards set up by English Heritage, just over 1 mile (1.6 km) further on, at the Coaley Peak picnic site, a popular spot for pulling off the road to picnic and enjoy the views. Opposite this viewpoint is the entrance to **Woodchester Park**, set in another secret Cotswold valley. Few people have been to the valley over the last 100 years, although that situation is likely to change now that the land has been acquired by the National Trust, who promise to make the area more accessible. There is a small car park at the entrance to the park and from here you can walk for miles to look at the plants and wildlife (tel: 01452 814213 for details; open daily 9am–6pm, or dusk in winter). Alternatively you can visit ★★ **Woodchester Mansion**, a striking 19th-century house that sits a third of the way down the 3-mile (5-km) long valley (tel: 01453 750455; open Easter–Oct, on the first weekend in every month, on bank holiday weekends including Mon and on Sat and Sun in Aug, Sept and early Oct; http://web.ukonline.co.uk/mansionoffice).

Visitors are given a guided tour of the house, which was begun in 1854. It was based on a design by Pugin, and the house is a fusion of French Gothic and traditional Cotswold styles. Before the house was completed, the builders were taken off to work on another project. They left their tools behind, expecting to return, but never did. The house remains frozen in time, a mid-Victorian building site with ladders and scaffolding still in place. Few rooms are plastered, so you can study the methods used to construct fireplaces, vaults and arches. Visitors interested in the practicalities of stone architecture will have a field day here, while others can just relax and absorb the special atmosphere of this bat and owl-haunted spot.

From Woodchester Park, the best route back to Tetbury is via Nymsfield, Kingscote and Beverston. It is well worth stopping in ★ **Beverston** to look at the church with its weatherworn Saxon carving of the Risen Christ on the tower, and its fine 13th-century nave. Next door is 13th-century Beverston Castle. The building is privately owned but it opens under the National Gardens Scheme on occasions in summer. Some 2 miles (3 km) north is ★★ **Chavenage House** (tel: 01666 502329; open May–Sept, Thur, Sun and Bank Holidays, 2–5pm; additionally Easter Sun/Mon), an E-shaped Elizabethan house, full of 16th- and 17th-century furniture and tapestries.

Beverston carving of the Risen Christ

Remains of Beverston Castle and adjoining house

From cloth-making to brewing

Stroud town centre

Route 3

Stroud and the Mill Valleys

Stroud – Nailsworth – Amberley – Minchinhampton – Avening – Cherington – Frampton Mansell – Bisley – Slad – Painswick – Haresfield Beacon – Standish – Leonard Stanley – King's Stanley – Selsley
See map page 16

The steep sided valleys around Stroud, with their fast-running streams, provided the ideal conditions for woollen mills in the 18th century, when cloth production ceased to be a cottage industry and became a factory-based process. Many of the mills constructed at this time looked as grand as stately homes, and some have survived, though most of these have been put to other uses. A few continue to produce high-quality cloth. Some open to the public on Wednesdays in summer for guided tours and demonstrations of working historic machinery (tel: 01453 766273 for further details).

★ **Stroud** was the centre of the industry, and it still has the feel of an industrial town. Much of the centre has been pedestrianised, and there are several small speciality shops to explore. Town trail leaflets can be obtained from the Tourist Information Centre in the Subscription Rooms, a handsome classical building of 1833, built as its name says by public subscription as a concert hall and art gallery. It still performs this role, especially during the annual Stroud Festival, held in September.

Also of interest is the Farmer's Market, one of the best in the area, held in Cornhill on the first and third Saturdays of each month. Stroud's **Museum in the Park**, in Stratford Park (tel: 01453 763394), opened in 2001.

Stroud's outskirts sprawl along the valleys of the River Frome and the Nailsworth Brook. As a result, once separate mill communities have now merged into one conurbation. Heading south for Nailsworth, you pass Rooksmoor Mills (1820), Woodchester Mill and, finest of all with its French-château-style clocktower, Ebley Mill (now home to Stroud District Council). The latter was built in 1818 and extended by G F Bodley, the church architect, in 1865 *(see Selsley, page 33, for more on Bodley)*.

In ★ **Nailsworth**, the mill theme continues in Market Street, with its late 18th-century Clothiers Arms and millworkers' cottages. Non-conformism came early to these valleys, and Chestnut Hill has a fine Quaker Meeting House of 1689. At the bottom of the valley, Egypt Mills (now a restaurant) was a corn mill that was later used for cloth dyeing, while on the B4014 Avening Road Ruskin Mill is now a craft centre (guided tours by appointment, tel: 01453 832571) with a coffee shop serving organic food and an exhibition gallery showing the work of violin and cabinet makers, jewellers and sculptors, stained-glass restorers and rug makers.

Nailsworth

From Nailsworth, very steep roads climb to the extensive limestone grasslands of Minchinhampton Common. Heading for Amberley, you will pass through the one-street hamlet of ★ **Watledge**, the last home of W. H. Davies, who wrote about his wanderings in Britain and America in *Autobiography of a Super-tramp* (1908), and penned the immortal couplet: 'What is this life if, full of care, We have no time to stand and stare.' ★ **Amberley** is where the Victorian novelist, Maria Craik, wrote much of her novel, *John Halifax, Gentleman* (1856), setting chapters against the background of the local mills. Unfenced roads lead across the common, a popular spot for picnics, kite-flying and horse-riding in summer. Parts of the common are rich in rare limestone wildflowers in summer, including harebells, rockrose, common spotted and pyramidal orchids and stemless thistle.

Following signs for Minchinhampton, you pass the ditches and banks known as the Bulwarks, thought to have been defences hastily thrown up in the 1st century AD by local Iron-Age tribes in an attempt to halt the westward advance of the Romans.

★★ **Minchinhampton** was another prosperous wool town, and the scores of ancient tracks that converge here were used by packhorses bringing wool for sale from nearby farms. The pillared Market Hall (1698) has survived, surrounded by fine 17th- and 18th-century houses and hotels. The church spire, oddly truncated, was in danger of collapsing so it was reduced in height in 1563 and given a stone coronet. The glorious south transept is

The pillared Market Hall

a triumph of the 14th-century Decorated style, with a lovely rose window and unusual stone scissor-bracing.

Heading southeast to Avening, the road skirts the boundary to Gatcombe Park, home of the Princess Royal. ★ **Avening** was another village that prospered on the cottage-based industry of skilled spinners and weavers. The fine ★★ **church**, of Saxon origin, contains a monument to Henry Brydges (died 1615) who was a notorious pirate, smuggler and highwayman until he married the daughter of a prosperous Avening clothier. The next village, ★ **Cherington**, has several more 18th-century clothiers' houses, distinguished buildings of stone with moulded eaves, architraves and cornices.

Clothier's house

From Cherington, a narrow road heads northeast, skirting Aston Down airfield, a favourite spot for launching gliders, and crossing the limestone plateau to descend into another valley system at ★ **Frampton Mansell**. There are fine views from Frampton's pretty neo-Norman church (1844) over the Golden Valley – in autumn the beech trees that clothe the valley's sides turn to gold.

Exploring the towpath

Frampton is a good spot to leave the car to explore the ★★ **canal towpath** in the valley bottom. The Thames and Severn Canal was built to link the River Severn (at Upper Framilode) with the River Thames (at Inglesham Lock). Completed in the year of the French Revolution (1789), it won plaudits from *The Times*, which hailed its construction as a stupendous achievement and a sign of Britain's stability by contrast with France's turmoil. The canal's working life was shortlived, however, because water continually leaked into the porous limestone, especially in the rock-cut tunnel which begins just east of here at Sapperton. In 1876 the Great Western Railway, whose track still runs parallel, bought the canal to prevent any rival company building another track along its course. Since then the canal has been left to nature, and walking the towpath will bring you face to face with moorhens, coots and grebes, dank lock basins alive with midges, sunny pools where dragon and damsel flies hunt for prey and bogs fragrant with watermint or musk. Enjoy this natural wilderness while it lasts. The Thames and Severn Canal Restoration Trust has financial backing to restore the canal in full working order – though it may take a decade or more.

Chalford mill and roundhouse

A welcome watering hole

If you head west along the canal you will pass natural lakes formed by the River Frome which runs alongside the canal for much of its length. In ★ **Chalford**, there are several historic mills, grouped around the former wharf, as well as a canal roundhouse, once occupied by the lengthman whose job was to maintain a length of the canal. Heading east, you will pass the Daneway Inn *(see Food and Drink, page 70)* before reaching the Sapperton end of the ★ **canal tunnel**, framed by an imposing classical portal.

From here, boats would be propelled the 2½ miles (4 km) through the tunnel to the Coates end by leggers, who lay on their backs and 'walked' along the tunnel walls.

If you don't want to walk too far, you can also see the tunnel entrance by visiting ★ **Sapperton**, and taking the footpath that heads downhill from the churchyard. Sapperton is built on a series of terraces overlooking the Golden Valley, and there are several good walks from the village, including the woodland path to Pinbury Park (gardens occasionally open under the National Gardens Scheme), the former home of John Masefield, and the place where Ernest Barnsley, Sidney Barnsley and Ernest Gimson first set up their Cotswold arts-and-crafts furniture-making workshops. All three are buried in the churchyard at Sapperton. The ★★ **church** itself, rebuilt at the beginning of the reign of Queen Anne, has big round-headed windows and pews made from Jacobean carved woodwork recycled when Sapperton House was demolished in 1730. Also of note are two fine Renaissance tombs, one to Sir Henry Poole (died 1616) and the other to Sir Robert Atkyns (died 1711), author of the first history of Gloucestershire, which he is holding.

At **Daneway**, in the valley below Sapperton, the steep hillside to the north of the pub is covered in grassy tussocks indicating the presence of old ants' nests, characteristic of unimproved Cotswold grassland. These fields, known as the ★★ **Daneway Banks**, now form part of a Gloucestershire Wildlife Trust reserve where you can see several varieties of orchid in summer.

A steep road runs west of the Banks and through beech woodland to the delightful village of ★★ **Bisley**, where footpaths thread their way between drystone walls sheltering many colourful cottage gardens in the vicinity of the fine 15th-century church. Thomas Keble (brother of John Keble, the Oxford Movement founder, vicar here from 1827 until his death in 1875) introduced the annual well-dressing ceremony held on Ascension Day, based on the spring-fed stone tanks in the lane south of the church.

The novelist Jilly Cooper has her home in this village, while the poet and novelist Laurie Lee lived most of his life in next-door ★ **Slad Valley**, whose delights he celebrated in *Cider with Rosie* (1959). To reach secluded Slad Valley, take the Stroud road out of Bisley, but turn right on the edge of the village down the narrow lane signposted to Elcombe. The road passes a disused quarry, now a Gloucestershire Wildlife Trust reserve with 11 species of orchid, adders, lizards, butterflies and rare grasshoppers.

From Slad it is a short drive to ★★★ **Painswick**, often described as the 'Queen of the Cotswolds' because of its elegant and harmonious groups of classically inspired

Bisley village

Painswick church gate

Painswick Rococo Garden

Haresfield Beacon

Cotswold stone houses. This, too, was a wool town, and the Painswick Brook, at the bottom of the valley, has several former fulling mills, now converted to apartments. The valley sides once supported fields of woad, grown to produce clothing dyes. The magnificent ★★ **churchyard** is famous both for the 99 topiary yews, which form a series of avenues leading to the church, and for the unusual collection of tea-caddy and table tombs. These are mostly the work of 18th-century masons, and they are carved with all kinds of baroque decorative devices, including cherubs, fruit and flower swags, pie crust frills, scrolls and shells. The church contains a number of curiosities, including graffiti carved into a pillar in the north nave by an imprisoned Puritan soldier during the 1643 siege of the village. It quotes from Edmund Spenser's *The Faerie Queene* – 'Be bolde, be bolde, be not too bold.'

On the northern outskirts of Painswick, on the B44073 Gloucester Road, is the entrance to the ★★ **Painswick Rococo Garden** (tel: 01452 813204; open Jan–Oct, daily 11am–5pm, Nov, Wed–Sun 11am–5pm). A rare survivor from the early 18th century, it represents the transition in styles from the formal to the natural landscape schools of gardening. Dotted with temples and gazebos, the garden enjoys a naturally dramatic setting in a sheltered combe, with woodland on all sides. The garden is at its most breathtaking in late January/early February when snowdrops appear.

Just north of the garden, there is a choice of viewpoints. At ★★ **Painswick Beacon**, the view across the Severn valley takes in the Welsh mountains in the distance, while below are the ditches and banks of an Iron-Age hillfort. Bearing left just after the beacon will take you in a big loop, via the viewpoint at Cud Hill, to the village of Edge, and then on to ★★ **Haresfield Beacon**. Here the views to the south look over a patchwork of dairy farms and orchards to the silvery Severn, while to the north they stretch along the escarpment to Cheltenham and beyond.

Descending from here into the flat vale comes as an anticlimax, though there are a couple more notable sites to see on the return journey to Stroud. ★ **Haresfield** is where the Tailor of Gloucester, John Prichard, lived later in life as a schoolmaster (*see page 20*). The church has some good monuments inside and fine table tombs outside. The same is true of ★ **Standish** church, where the boldly carved skeletons and cherubs have escaped weather erosion. Inside there is a splendidly painted memorial to Sir Henry Winston, an ancestor of Sir Winston Churchill, and there is a 16th-century parish house alongside, now used as offices by the Gloucestershire Wildlife Trust. From Stonehouse, you cross the 18th-century Stroudwater Canal on

Selsley church

the way to ★ **Leonard Stanley**, where the parish church once served the monks of the Augustinian priory of St Leonard, founded in 1121. The very fine Romanesque capitals of the chancel depict the Nativity and Mary Magdalene washing the feet of Jesus with her hair. The original parish church (of Saxon origin) still survives in use as a cart shed in the adjacent farmyard, along with a 14th-century monastic barn and fishpond (they can be seen from the western end of the churchyard). Anyone interested in barns should also visit ★ **Frocester**, just 1 mile (1.6 km) east, where the magnificent Great Barn (1300) survives in its original form (ask at the farm to visit).

In ★ **King's Stanley**, straddling the River Frome, the magnificent Stanley Mill has been restored with funding from English Heritage. It is a pioneering example of fireproof construction: iron and brick were the main materials used when it was built in 1815, and wood was banned altogether, even for the floors.

Heading south from King's Stanley, a narrow road climbs through Middleyard to ★★ **Selsley** and one of the Cotswolds' most delightful Victorian churches. The church, and the adjacent house, were built by Sir Samuel Marling, owner of Ebley Mill whose French-style clocktower is visible in the valley as you look to the right across the churchyard. Marling had once visited the village of Marlengo in the Austrian Tyrol, because of its similarity to his own name. He decided Selsley was sufficiently alpine in feel to justify the construction of a church based on that at Marlengo – the result is this striking building designed by the architect G.F. Bodley in 1862. The stained glass here was the first to be designed by the then newly formed firm of Morris & Co. William Morris, Philip Webb, Ford Madox Brown, Dante Gabriel Rossetti and Edward Burne-Jones all had a hand in the design of the lively and colourful Creation window that fills the west gable.

Detail of the Creation window

Route 4

Cirencester, the Duntisbournes and Churn Valley

Cirencester – Daglingworth – Duntisbourne Rouse and Abbots – Miserden – Prinknash – Birdlip, Crickley Hill and Leckhampton country parks – Coberley – Cowley – Elkstone – Rendcomb – North Cerney – Bagendon – Baunton *See map page 16*

Cirencester

Corinium Museum

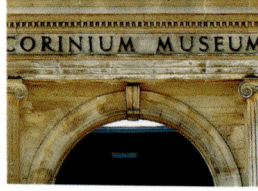

A glance at a map reveals that ★★★ **Cirencester** sits at the hub of a network of Roman roads – the Fosse Way, the Ermin Way, Akeman Street, the White Way – and that Cirencester itself retains the rectilinear street plan of a Roman town. Founded in the 1st century AD as Corinium Dobunorum, it was the second largest city in Roman Britain, exceeded only by London in size.

Gardeners in Cirencester are used to turning up Roman pottery and lumps of mosaic, and any building project must be preceded by archaeological investigation, the fruits of which are displayed in the excellent ★★ **Corinium Museum** in Park Street (tel: 01285 655611; open Mon–Sat 10am–5pm, Sun 2–5pm). With one of England's richest collections of Romano-British antiquities, the Corinium Museum has been able to create several tableaux depicting daily life in Roman times, with a full-size dining room, kitchen, mosaic workshop and a garden. There are Roman legionary tombstones of outstanding quality and richly carved capitals, as well as endearing altars devoted to the local gods, the so-called *genii cucullati* ('hooded spirits'). Best of all from an aesthetic point of view are the mosaics, ranging from accomplished depictions of Roman mythological figures to the naturalistic rendering of local wildlife displayed by the Hare Mosaic. The museum, which also has displays on the Cotswold wool industry, monasticism and the Civil War, has a good bookshop where you can buy trail leaflets covering every aspect of this architecturally and historically rich town.

Turning left out of the museum will take you up Black Jack Street, past the Edwardian tiled shopfront of Jesse Smith the butchers, to the ★★ **parish church**, with its magnificent tower and two-storey fan-vaulted porch opening onto the broad and handsome market place (market on Mon and Fri). Inside the church, the riches range from the precious Anne Boleyn cup (1535) and the lovely 15th-century wine-glass pulpit to numerous fine funerary monuments and brasses and the wall paintings and fan-vaulting of St Catherine's Chapel.

If the tower is open at the time of your visit, it is well worth the effort of climbing to the top for a view of Cirencester Mansion, built by the first Earl Bathurst

Parish church

between 1714–18, and hidden from view at street level by the world's tallest yew hedge. Beyond the mansion are the broad tree-lined avenues of the 30,000-acre (12,150-hectare) Cirencester Park, which is open to the public. This is an early example of English landscape gardening, laid out by Bathurst with the aid of his friend, the poet Alexander Pope. The walk to the park entrance passes through several of Cirencester's most handsome streets: Dollar Street, Coxwell Street, Thomas Street and Cecily Hill all lined by houses of 17th- and 18th-century wool merchants.

Whichever way you journey out of Cirencester, you quickly pass into fine countryside dotted with farming hamlets. Heading north, through Stratton, turn left to reach the deep tree-shaded lanes of the Dunt valley, stopping first at ★ **Daglingworth** where the church has unusually well-preserved Saxon carvings of the Crucifixion. Most of the churches around Cirencester are of late Saxon origin (10th century) but most have been rebuilt several times over as architectural fashions changed. One that retains much of its original appearance is the tiny church at ★ **Duntisbourne Rouse**, set on a steep bank above the Dunt, where the nave is Saxon, the chancel early Norman and the little saddle-backed tower dates from the 15th century.

Heading on through Middle Duntisbourne and Duntisbourne Leer, there are several idyllic farmyard groups to be seen if you divert off to the right to the bottom of the valley. In each case the farmyard buildings are grouped around the river, which forms a ford. Between Duntisbourne Leer and Duntisbourne Abbots, the river actually flows down the main road for a distance of some 30 yds (27 metres), deliberately diverted in this way to create a water lane to wash the clay off the wheels of carts and

Daglingworth church

Daglingworth garden detail

Duntisbourne Abbots

Gravestone with death heads

Misarden Park Gardens and Nursery

the fetlocks of horses as they returned from the fields. For most of the year, the lane is too deep for cars to negotiate, but walkers can follow the raised stone-flagged footpath that runs alongside.

★ **Duntisbourne Abbots' church** sits at the centre of a village on a plateau surrounded by stone cottages built on terraces cut into the hillside. Eighteenth-century tombs carved with cherubs and skulls line the churchyard path and the door retains its original 15th-century ironwork and closing ring.

From the valley of the Dunt, head eastwards to the lovely wooded valley of the upper Frome, aiming for ★★ **Miserden**. The church here is Saxon, and the south aisle contains two outstanding monuments. One is topped by a painted stone effigy of William Kingston (died 1614), with a wonderfully naturalistic heraldic goat at his feet, chewing on the branch of a tree. The other, crisply carved in alabaster with careful attention to every lacy detail of the clothing, depicts Sir William Sandys (died 1640), his wife, Margaret Culpeper (died 1644) and their large family. A humbler tomb in the churchyard, on the right of the path as you leave the church, has a brass plaque that well illustrates the lost art of epitaph composition. It marks the grave of a shepherd named Samuel Horrell (died 1807) and reads:

> *From youth through life the sheep was all his care*
> *And harmless as the flock his manners were*
> *On earth he held the faith to Christians given*
> *In hope to join the fold of Christ in heaven*

Manicured Miserden is an estate village, and the big house lies at the opposite end from the church, signposted ★★ **Misarden Park Gardens and Nursery** (tel: 01285 821303; gardens open Apr–Sept, Tues–Thur 10am–5pm; nursery open daily except Mon). The house is Elizabethan in origin, built by the Sandys family and extended with a Renaissance-style loggia and east wing by Sir Edwin Lutyens. The gardens are set on a series of terraces with extensive southward views down the beech-clad Frome valley. The outline of the garden, with a central walk lined by ancient yew hedges clipped into dome-shaped battlements, dates from the 17th century. The walled garden contains fine displays of roses and clematis, while the lower terraces are planted more informally with flowering trees and shrubs, and masses of naturalised bulbs.

From Miserden the road north passes through **Whiteway**, an unusual hamlet of single-storey timber houses built by the grandparents of the present occupants who came here as early pioneers of self-sufficiency – though not in the 1960s, as you might expect, but in 1898, inspired by the ideas of the Russian novelist and Christian mystic, Count Leo Tolstoy.

Contine through ★ **Cranham**, where the church has a pair of sheep shears carved amongst the gargoyles on the splendid tower. You then reach **Prinknash Abbey** (pronounced 'Prinage'), where another group of self-sufficient Christians settled amongst the glorious beech woods three decades later, in 1928. The Catholic Benedictines who founded the monastery took over a 16th-century house that had once belonged to the abbots of Gloucester, and they began extending it in 1939, using stone and wood quarried and felled on the site.

Cranham church

To pay for the work, the monks founded ★★ **Prinknash Pottery** (tel: 01452 812066; open for tours daily 9am–4.30pm). Here they created the distinctive black lustre-glazed pottery that has become their trademark, though they now produce a very wide range of different products that are sold in the gift shop. The new abbey, completed in 1972, is a distinctive modern building. Visitors can enter the fine chapel with its outstanding stained-glass, designed by one of the monks.

Prinknash pots

In the monastic grounds there is a ★★ **Bird and Deer Park**, which is run as a separate enterprise (tel: 01452 812727; open daily 10am–5pm). Here, set amongst woodland, is a series of ponds, bridges and islands where swans, ducks and wild geese, not to mention tame fallow deer, African pygmy goats and large carp, will try to persuade you to feed them.

There's more than just pottery

Dropping over the edge from Prinknash, it takes no time at all to descend from the glorious beech woods to the built-up outskirts of Gloucester. Passing through Upton St Leonards and Hucclecote, pick up the old A417 to Brockworth, then follow the signs for ★ **Great Witcombe Roman Villa** (open daylight hours). The villa enjoys a lovely setting, sheltered by the escarpment to the east, but with open views to the west. A spring still feeds the site and was the reason why the villa was situated here at all – though even in Roman times the walls of the villa had to be buttressed to prevent subsidence caused by the unstable and wet subsoil. The villa remains consist of living rooms and bath houses, plus some mosaics and hypocausts (underfloor heating systems) that are hidden inside timber sheds and kept locked for much of the time (you can telephone to enquire about occasional open days when they can be viewed).

If you are here in summer, it is worth exploring the footpaths around the villa, for the wet meadows support many wildflowers, including drifts of orchids and ragged robin. From the villa you can also see Cooper's Hill, to the west, the site of the traditional cheese-rolling contest held every Whit Monday. This may have begun as a ceremony to stake out grazing rights, and it involves chasing a Double Gloucester cheese, protected by a disk-shaped wooden case, as it rolls at speed down a steep grassy slope. This is no sport for the fainthearted (limbs are frequently broken), but the first to catch the cheese gets to take it home.

If you are keen on seeking out rare wildflowers, or if you just want to enjoy a walk along the breezy tops of the Cotswold escarpment, you can choose from the three country parks in the vicinity. ★ **Birdlip Country Park** is reached by heading up steep Birdlip Hill and turning left in Birdlip itself. Several barrows (the heaps of earth that mark prehistoric tombs) dot the short-cropped grass on this hill, including the barrow from which the Birdlip mirror *(see Gloucester City Museum and Art Gallery, page 21)* was excavated. Wildflowers to be found here include wild thyme and milkwort, pyramidal orchids and various vetches that attract small blue and brown butterflies.

A little further along the scarp is ★★ **Crickley Hill Country Park**, reached from the B4070 Leckhampton Road. The visitor centre here has displays charting the history of the Iron Age hillfort that occupies the western edge of the hill (tel: 01452 863170; open daily 9am–5pm). Having absorbed all the archaeological information, children can run off and play at being Celtic warriors, or scour the exposed rocks for fossils.

Fossil hunting at the ★★ **Leckhampton Country Park**, on the eastern side of the same B4070 road, has unfortunately reached nuisance proportions, and there is scarcely an exposed rock face that has not been defaced by pointless and destructive hammering. There are several exposures here, showing the various oolitic beds that make up the Cotswolds, from the top layer of ragstone (used since Celtic times as a walling and housebuilding material) to the deeper layers of freestone (used from the 17th-century onwards for smooth-fronted classical buildings). In fact, Leckhampton Hill served as the main quarry for the Greek-Revival buildings of Cheltenham *(see page 43)*, the town that lies in the plain below. Following the main path through the country park you will find a prominent column of rock left by late 18th-century quarrymen known as the Devil's Chimney.

The back road from the country park leads to the ★ **Seven Springs** crossroads. Turn right on the A436 Gloucester road to find the actual springs, which are on the right-hand side of the road just after the junction. Litter sadly mars what could be an idyllic spot where clear spring waters bubble out from beneath a shelf of rock at several different points, forming the source of the River

Views at Birdlip Country Park

A closer look

Churn. There are those who believe this is the true source of the Thames: certainly the Churn is a considerably longer river than its rivals for the title from its source to the point where it meets the Thames at Cricklade; for that reason alone Seven Springs ought to be considered the fount of England's longest river. Instead that honour goes to a dreary patch of dried-up mud in a field near Kemble.

The delightful river Churn contributes to the charm of the villages that it passes through. At ★ **Coberley** the river forms a marsh that is bright with the flowers of marsh marigolds, yellow flags, watermint and purple loosestrife, depending on the season. The church, invisible from the road, is reached by pushing open a doorway in an ancient barn and walking across a farmyard. Inside there are 13th- and 14th-century monuments to knights in chain mail armour, and one to the mother of thrice-times mayor of London, Dick Whittington.

At ★ **Cowley**, the river is dammed to form a series of cascades and a fish-filled lake fronting **Cowley Manor**. This handsome mid-19th century building, in the Italian style, was built for Sir James Horlick, co-inventor, with his brother, of the famous beverage. The gardens have been replanted with drifts of naturalised bulbs and perennials by the well-known local garden designer, Noel Kingsbury. At present, the manor is being converted into a luxury hotel, but it is likely that the gardens will be open to the public again in due course – in the meantime they can be glimpsed if you visit the small church in the grounds.

Due south of Cowley, it is worth diverting from the Churn valley to visit one of the most celebrated churches in the Cotswolds. Quirky ★★ **Elkstone** has Romanesque beast heads forming a guard around the south doorway to keep demons at bay, and a tympanum showing Christ seated

Coberley river and meadows

Cowley Manor and gardens

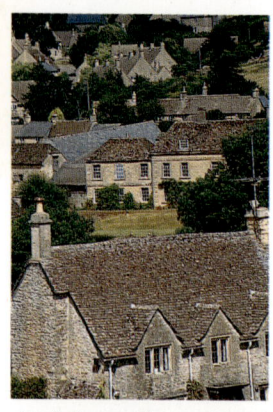

in majesty. Inside are bold chevroned arches and dragon head stops, and (uniquely) a pigeon loft above the chancel, reached via a stairway near the pulpit.

★★ **Rendcomb's church** is like Fairford's *(see page 59)* in miniature scale, sharing such features as an exceptionally fine and complete wooden chancel screen and some good stained glass, both dating to the early decades of the 16th century. The link is that John Tame built Fairford church, while his son, Sir Edmund Tame, built Rendcomb church; it is likely that the same craftsmen worked on both churches. Rendcomb also has an outstanding Romanesque stone font carved with figures representing 11 of the Apostles; the space for Judas is left blank. The church doubles as a chapel for the next-door school, which occupies another handsome Italianate house of the mid-19th century.

North Cerney village and church

A short way down the valley, ★★ **North Cerney** church is packed with interest. On the outside are two large pieces of graffiti, perhaps doodled in an idle moment by the masons who restored the Norman church after a fire in the 15th century. One shows a leopard and another a mythological manticore (with the head of a man and the body of a beast), both similar to drawings found in popular bestiaries of the period. Inside is a lovely rood screen supporting a figure of Christ carved in Italy around 1600, reminding us of the way many parish churches would have looked before the iconoclasts of the Reformation period systematically removed these features.

Up the hill from the church, ★★ **Cerney House Gardens** (tel: 01285 831205; open by appointment only) has spring bulbs in abundance, a working kitchen and herb garden and a splendid walled garden full of herbaceous plants and roses. If you are here at the right time, you can watch the milking of the goats that produce Cerney cheese, and buy stocks of homemade ice-cream, goat's milk or cheese.

Less than 1 mile (1.6 km) southwest of Cerney is ★ **Bagendon**, surrounded by earthworks marking the boundary of the principal settlement of the Dobunni, the Iron-Age tribe after whom Roman Cirencester (Corinium Dobunorum) was named. From being the capital of a thriving Celtic community, with a mint and well-developed metal-working industry, Bagendon has become a quiet backwater with a pretty Saxon church and Norman saddleback tower containing a priest's chamber.

One last Churn-valley church is worth a call before you return to Cirencester: ★ **Baunton** glories in a huge 14th-century St Christopher painted on the north wall. Fabulous fish swim around the saint's feet and a ship rides at anchor in one corner, while a fisherman sits on one bank and a hermit with a lamp stands by a chapel on the other.

Route 5

Cheltenham and the Cotswold Escarpment

Cheltenham – Cleeve Hill – Winchcombe – Sudeley Castle – Hailes Abbey – Stanway – Stanton – Buckland – Snowshill – Broadway

Regency Cheltenham

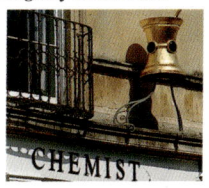

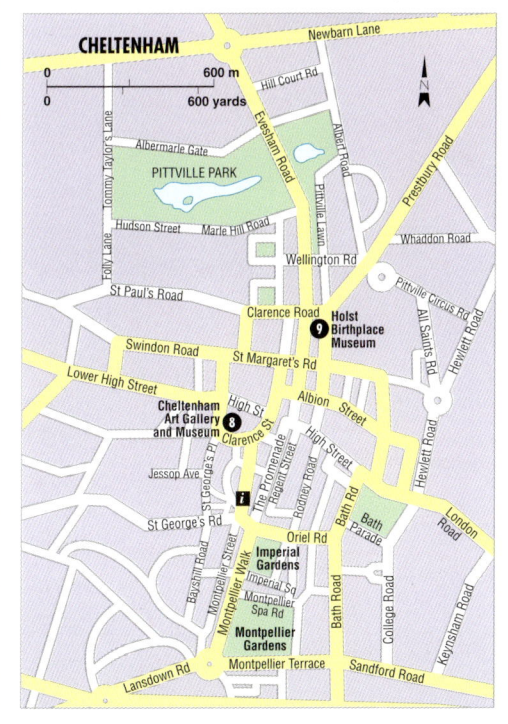

★★★ **Cheltenham**'s coat of arms features pigeons because it was these birds, pecking at salt grains in a meadow outside the town, that led to the discovery of the mineral springs that were to make the town famous. The springs were discovered in 1716, but it was not until George II visited the town in 1788 that high society began to adopt Cheltenham as a summer resort.

In the three decades following the royal visit, the population increased seven-fold and £5 million was invested in speculative development. Row upon row of Regency houses, with fine wrought-iron balconies and fanlights, were erected around the Pitville Pump Room, with its graceful dome and pillared portico modelled on the temple of Illisus in Athens.

The focus of Cheltenham has shifted somewhat since the 18th century, so that most visitors

ROUTES 5-8

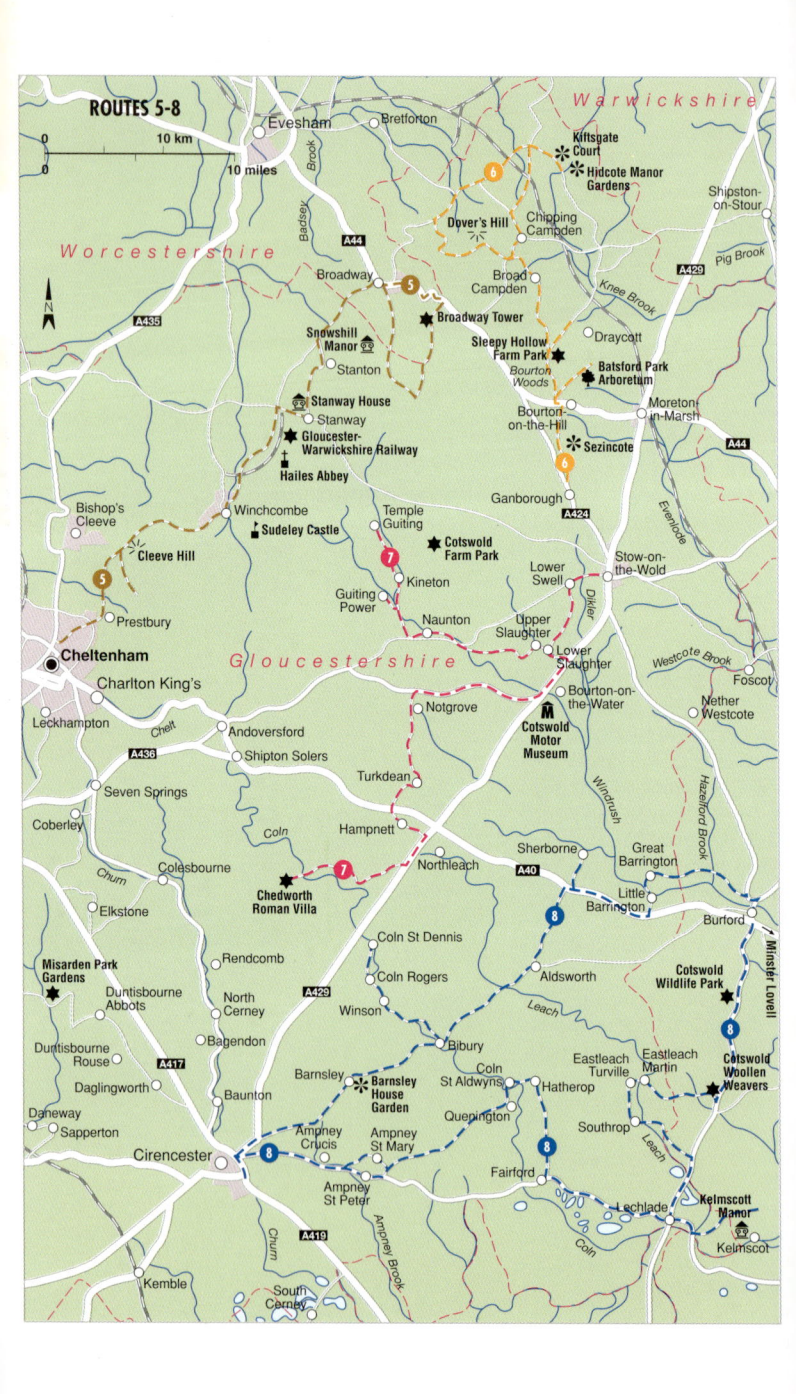

now arrive in the commercial heart, in one of the car parks that lie near to the pedestrianised High Street, with its big stores, such as Marks & Spencer and Virgin Records *(see Shopping, page 72)*. To rediscover Regency Cheltenham, it is best to head for the Promenade, or the **Prom**, as it is known locally. Noble Greek-Revival terraces line one side of this broad leafy avenue, where fortunes were once gambled away in smart gentlemen's clubs. Opposite are the tempting plate-glass windows of smart shops and the Cavendish House department store. Neptune, god of the sea, dominates the splendid fountain at the upper end of the Prom, and nearby is a statue of Cheltenham-born Edward Wilson, one of the explorers who died on Scott's ill-fated Antarctic expedition of 1912.

Making a splash on the Prom

If you continue up the promenade, you will pass the elegant Town Hall on the left (now a major concert and festival venue) surrounded by the colourful Imperial Gardens, full of bright flowers in the traditional municipal bedding style. The luxurious Queen's Hotel, with award-winning restaurants, closes the vista as you look across the manicured lawns of the gardens. On the opposite side of the road is elegant Montpellier Walk (1825), with female caryatids (inspired by those of the Acropolis in Athens) and a fascinating mix of antique shops delicatessans, designer boutiques, and pavement cafes. Coming back down Montepellier Street, one block to the west, you will pass Cheltenham Ladies College, the renowned educational establishment founded in 1854.

Montpellier Walk

Passing along Royal Well Road and the stucco-fronted terraces of Royal Crescent, you will find the excellent ★★ **Cheltenham Art Gallery and Museum** ❽ to the left, in Clarence Street (tel: 01242 237431; open Mon–Sat 10am–5.20pm Sun 2–4.20pm). The museum is packed with material on the history of Cheltenham and its people. There are displays of Chinese and Indian-inspired house furnishings that were in fashion amongst the army officers and colonial civil servants who favoured Cheltenham as a place to retire. By contrast there is a comprehensive display of furniture made by members of the Cotswolds arts-and-crafts movement *(see page 66)*, some fine paintings and much material on local wildlife and archaeology.

Behind the museum, footpaths lead between grey tombstones past the parish church, one of Cheltenham's few pre-18th century buildings, hidden behind the shops of the High Street. Turn right down the High Street, then fourth left, up Winchcombe Street, then left again to find 4 Clarence Road. Here you will find the modest house in which Gustav Holst spent the early part of his life, now the ★★ **Holst Birthplace Museum** ❾ (tel: 01242 524846; open Tues–Sat 10am–4pm). The house is furnished in appropriate style, with late-Victorian and Edwardian

Holst Museum

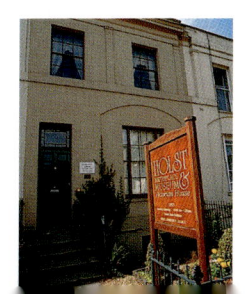

interiors telling us as much about life at the turn of the 20th century as about Holst himself, the composer of the ever-popular *Planets Suite*.

From this point it is a short walk north to the Pitville Pump Room, set amidst the manicured lawns of Pitville Park. Here, under the Pump Room's dome, you can sample the heavily mineralised water that brought fame to Cheltenham. It tastes so salty that you will only want one sip, but it is said to be good for constipation, rheumatism and gout, amongst other bodily disorders.

Cheltenham remains very much a fashionable shopping centre and is noted for its annual festivals of folk music (February), jazz (May), classical music (July) and literature (October). For details of all these festivals see the website www.cheltenhamfestivals.co.uk The town is never more festive than during March when members of the racing fraternity descend on the town for the Cheltenham Gold Cup and the Champion Hurdle, the premier events of the National Hunt calendar. The racecourse is at **Prestbury**, some 2 miles (3.2 km) north of the town; if you cannot spend a day at the races, you can always visit the ★ **The Hall of Fame** and learn about the history of the sport (tel: 01242 513014; open Mon–Fri 9.30am–4.30pm).

Beyond Prestbury the B4632 climbs the Cotswold escarpment to reach **Cleeve Hill**, where car parks allow you to pull off the road and walk up to the trig point on the summit. Here you are 1,040 ft (317 metres) above sea level, and the views on a clear day take in every range of hills for a distance of 30 miles (50 km) westwards. The highest point in the Cotswolds, at 1,080 ft (330 metres), lies 2 miles (3.2 km) south on Cleeve Common, but at only 43ft (13 metres) higher, it is probably not worth the walk.

A music festival is held in July

Cheltenham's elegant centre

Descending Cleeve Hill, you will soon reach the lovely town of ★★ **Winchcombe**, with its long main street and its church noted for its splendidly grotesque gargoyles. Inside the church are two stone tombs, claimed to be those of King Kenelf and his son, the boy martyr St Kenelm, said to have been murdered by his sister in AD 819 because of his fervent devotion to Christianity. The story was invented by monks at Winchcombe's Benedictine Abbey (of which no trace now remains above ground), but it drew plenty of pilgrims to the town and made the abbey one of the wealthiest in England in the Middle Ages.

Gargoyle on Winchcombe's church

Just beyond the church, a lane leads off to the right to ★★★ **Sudeley Castle** (tel: 01242 602308; open Apr–Oct, 10.30am–5.30pm; rest of year 11am–5pm). The present castle dates from the 15th century, though it was deliberately ruined by Parliamentary forces during the Civil War. Left to decay for two centuries, it was made habitable again between 1837 and 1936.

Dressed for the part at Sudeley Castle

The castle's most famous resident was Catherine Parr (1512-48), the sixth wife of Henry VIII. Six weeks after becoming a widow, Catherine married Sudeley's owner, the Lord Admiral Seymour, and moved to the castle at Sudeley, though she only survived the king by a year: after giving birth to her only daughter, Mary, she died of puerperal fever, and was buried in Sudeley's chapel. During the Civil War, her original monument was lost, but there is now a fine alabaster tomb in the chapel, carved in 1859 with a serene effigy of the queen.

Surrounding the chapel are the romantic gardens first laid out by Emma Dent, who came to Sudeley on her marriage in 1852 and set about restoring the castle and its grounds. An indefatigable collector, she succeeded in furnishing the castle with an outstanding collection of Tudor and Carolean furnishings, paintings (including works by Parmigiano, Van Dyke and Rubens) and relics of the Civil War.

Sudeley Castle's gardens

If you take children to Sudeley, you may have difficulty dragging them away from the big adventure playground in the grounds. The offer of a ride on a steam train on the ★ **Gloucestershire–Warwickshire Railway** (tel: 01242 621405; open weekends Mar–Oct and daily during school holidays – telephone for a detailed timetable or see the website www.gwsr.plc.uk) might do the trick. This restored Great Western Railway line runs between Greet (1 mile/1.6 km north of Winchcombe town centre) and Toddington (4 miles/6 km northeast of Winchcombe), a 13-mile/21km round trip that includes the Greet tunnel.

You might catch sight of trains chuffing along the line as you head for ★★ **Hailes Abbey**, 2 miles (3.2 km) northeast of the town (tel: 01242 602398; open Apr–Sept daily 10am–6pm; Oct, 10am–5pm). The Cistercian abbey was

Hailes Abbey

Stanway House

founded in 1246 by King John's son, the Earl of Cornwall. His son, Edmund, donated a glass phial containing the Blood of Christ, guaranteeing a steady stream of pilgrims seeking a miraculous cure by touching the precious relic. The relic was declared a fake at the Dissolution, and the monastery was plundered for building materials. Little remains now except for footings. There is, however, an excellent museum containing finds from excavations that indicate how splendid the abbey once was. The parish church at Hailes is also worth a visit for the traces of wall paintings and the 13th-century encaustic tiles.

Two miles (3.2 km) north of Hailes is **Stanway** where, after turning a sharp bend into the village, you will be greeted by a wonderfully exuberant Jacobean gatehouse leading to ★★ **Stanway House** (tel: 01386 584469; open July–Aug, Tues and Thurs 2–5pm or by appointment). Even if the house is not open at the time of your visit, you can get a flavour of it from the churchyard. A majestic 14th-century tithe barn stands to the north of the church, while the house stands to the west. The house is more austere inside than you might expect, for it has escaped improvement and retains the feel of a 17th-century courthouse, with its period furnishings and family portraits. Pleasing gardens surround the house, complete with the remains of an 18th-century baroque water garden, with waterfalls, a fountain and a stone cascade running down the hillside to the lake.

As you explore the bedrooms at Stanway, think of the famous author James Barrie, who was a frequent visitor in the early 1900s. Moonlight flickering across his bedroom wall is said to have inspired him with the idea of the fairy Tinkerbell in *Peter Pan*. A keen cricketer, he also designed the thatched pavilion standing on staddle stones north of the village.

★ **Stanton** is an almost-too-perfect village of thatched stone cottages which have been beautifully maintained over the decades following the example set by the squire of Stanton Court in the early 20th century. Saddened by the loss of so many young men of the village in World War I, he also paid for the church to be restored by Sir Ninian Comper as a war memorial. Comper added the west gallery and the fine rood screen between 1918–1923. To appreciate the village fully, it is best to come on the weekend in summer (usually in July) when many of the gardens are open under the National Gardens Scheme.

Stanton stands in the lee of the Cotswold escarpment, and walkers can reach Snowshill easily enough by taking a short walk over the top and into the next valley. Visitors by car have to take a more circuitous route back through Stanway. ★★★ **Snowshill Manor** is a popular attraction, so expect what the National Trust calls 'serious overcrowding' if you go on summer Sundays or bank holiday weekends (tel: 01386 852410; open Apr–Oct, Wed–Sun 12–5pm; Jul–Aug also open Mon). The manor is the creation of the eccentric Charles Paget Wade, who devoted many years of his solitary life, 1919 to 1951, to restoring the handsome 15th–18th-century house and creating one of Gloucestershire's finest gardens. The arts-and-crafts influence in Wade's work is evident in the exposed timber roofs, the Tudor-style oak panelling carved by Wade himself using period tools, and the magpie collection of objects which fill the rooms. These are all treasured examples of skilled craftsmanship, from samurai armour to musical instruments, clocks and locally made weaving and spinning machines. The famous gardens, which were conceived by Wade as a series of outdoor rooms enclosed by walls and hedges, form a delightful maze around the old manor house.

Snowshill Manor

William Morris, the ultimate progenitor of the arts-and-crafts ethic, used to spend holidays not far from here in the Broadway Tower, set high on the Cotswold escarpment, some 3 miles (5 km) northeast of Snowshill. Today the tower stands at the centre of the ★ **Broadway Country Park**, with its animal enclosures (red deer and rare breeds of farm animal) and adventure playground (tel: 01386 852390; open Apr–Oct, daily 10.30am–5pm; Nov–Mar, Sat–Sun 11am–3pm). The tower was built in the late 18th century by the Earl of Coventry and on clear days enjoys views over 12 counties. Even if it is too hazy to see that far, the tower is well worth visiting for its exhibitions covering the history of the tower, sheep and wool farming in the Cotswolds and William Morris, who once lived in the tower.

The descent from the tower, by the steep escarpment road into ★★ **Broadway**, provides a dramatic introduction to this manicured village, with its crowded streets, its boutiques and art galleries, its tea shops, restaurants and shopping mall. Fine buildings also line both sides of the village street, including the imposing Lygon Arms Hotel, a Renaissance building restored and furnished by arts- and crafts devotees in the early 20th century. Furniture-making today is represented by the workshops of the late Gordon Russell, whose premises lie on the north side of the green. Broadway's **church**, not to be missed, lies a good mile (1.6 km) out of town to the south, next to the Jacobean Court House, whose ancient and bulbous yew trees spill over from the garden into the churchyard. The peaceful, mellow church, with its uneven tiled floor and rustic memorials, was left alone once a new church was built in Broadway in 1839, and as a result it feels like a place where time has almost stood still ever since.

Broadway's mellow charm

Route 6

Chipping Campden and the Gardens of the North Cotswolds

Chipping Campden – Dover's Hill – Hidcote Manor – Kiftsgate Court – Broad Campden – Blockley – Sezincote – Batsford Park – Cotswold Falconry Centre – Bourton House Garden – Moreton-in-Marsh – Sleepy Hollow Farm Park *See map page 42*

Chipping Campden: an idyllic Cotswold town

For many visitors, ★★★ **Chipping Campden** is the quintessential Cotswold town, although it is, in many respects, utterly untypical, not least in having been kept in a beautifully preserved state by the efforts of the Campden Trust. Formed back in 1929 by a group of local architects and craftsmen, the Trust has restored many properties, and it sets high standards for the appearance of the town. Telegraph and power cables are buried underground or brought into the backs of houses so that wires do not mar the appearance of the broad High Street, and intrusive modern shopfronts are not allowed.

Another unusual feature at Campden is the sheer variety of buildings in a plethora of different styles that have survived from all ages. One that visitors see first is the dramatic gatehouse to Campden Manor, built by Sir Baptist Hicks in 1613 in flamboyant Jacobean style, and then deliberately burned down by the Royalists during the Civil War to prevent it falling into the hands of the hated Parliamentarians. Hicks, himself a fierce Royalist, also built the fine block of almshouses opposite the manor gateway. Dating from 1612, the plan of the block makes the letter 'I', in honour of King James (or Iames, as the name was sometimes spelled).

Church of St James

Hicks (died 1629) has an imposing monument in Campden's ★★ **Church of St James**, possibly carved by the great English Renaissance sculptor Nicholas Stone. The nave of the church (built by the same masons as Northleach church) is a triumph of the Perpendicular style, with its slender octagonal columns supporting a lofty roof, lit by large clerestory windows. The church has a number of brasses dating from the time when Campden was one of the Cotswolds' main wool markets. In front of the altar is one dedicated to a merchant who thrived on this trade: William Grevel (died 1301) is described in his epitaph as 'the flower of the wool merchants of England'.

Grevel's House

The house that Grevel built in 1380 still survives in the High Street, on the right as you enter the street from Church Street; it is unmistakable because of its two-storeyed bay window. On the opposite side of the road is the stylish Bedfont House, a delightful classical building of the 1740s now beautifully cleaned and restored. Another building of note along the main street is the **Market Hall** of 1627, another gift to the town paid for by Sir Baptist Hicks. It looks like an Italian Renaissance loggia but with Cotswold-style gables.

A number of the shops in Campden are devoted to selling crafts and objects that exemplify good design (for example, Robert Welch's shop on the Lower High Street). This is, in part, a legacy of the Guild of Handicrafts that was set up in Campden in 1902 by C.R. Ashbee. Inspired by ideals of reviving craft traditions that gave men and women pride in their work, rather than making them merely adjuncts to machinery, Ashbee moved here from the Mile End Road with a group of East End families and set up a workshop in the old Silk Mill in Sheep Street. The ground floor of the mill has been turned into a small ★ **museum** devoted to Ashbee and his work (tel: 01386 841417; open daylight hours), and you can visit the silver workshop founded by one of Ashbee's followers, George Hart, on the floor above.

Market Hall of 1627

It is worth taking a stroll up ★ **Dover's Hill**, a mile northwest of the town. This spectacular natural amphitheatre provides views in every direction, down onto Campden to the southeast, to the Vale of Evesham to the northwest and over the Burnt Norton estate (which inspired T.S. Eliot's poem in the *Four Quartets*) to the north. This is also the setting for the Cotswold Olimpick Games, so called by Robert Dover after whom the hill is named. The eccentric Dover started the games in 1612 and they feature such rural sports as shin-kicking, climbing the greasy pole and duelling with backswords (a polite name for wooden cudgels), all designed to be a training in 'the manly sports for the harmless mirthe and jollitie of the neighbourhood'.

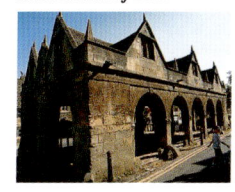

Chipping Campden

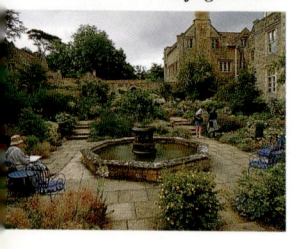

The games continued uninterrupted (except for a brief period during the Civil War) until 1852 when the rowdy behaviour of 'armed bands of beer-swilling Birmingham yahoos' got them banned. Revived in 1951, they now take place on the last weekend in May or the first in June, and are followed by a torchlit procession into Campden where the townspeople dance until late in the floodlit High Street.

For garden lovers, the real highlight of the day is to visit the celebrated ★★★ **Hidcote Manor Gardens** at Hidcote Bartrim, 3 miles (5 km) northeast of Chipping Campden (tel: 01684 855370; open Apr–Sept, daily 10.30am–6.30pm; closed Thurs and Fri in Apr, May, Aug and Sept; Oct, daily except Thurs and Fri 10.30am–5.30pm).

Hidcote Manor Gardens

These days there is something of a reaction against the kind of highly architectural garden that Hidcote pioneered, and young garden designers prefer a more naturalistic style, with a greater emphasis on plants grown in drifts, rather than using them to decorate outdoor rooms bounded by clipped yews and pleached limes. Few but the most hardened iconoclasts are immune to the charm of Hidcote in the flesh, however, and the garden will give encouragement and inspiration to anyone struggling to create their own patch of colour and wondering if it will ever look mature. Remember that this garden did not exist until 1907, created from an unpromising farmyard set high on a cold, exposed and windswept hill. The garden was still incomplete in 1948 when its creator, Lawrence Johnstone, handed it over to the National Trust.

There is another great garden to see just down the road. At the same time that Johnstone was devoting his life to Hidcote, Heather Muir was busy creating the garden at ★★★ **Kiftsgate Court** (tel: 01386 438777; open Apr–Sept, Wed, Thur, Sun and bank holidays 2–6pm; June–July, Wed, Thur, Sat and Sun noon-6pm). Kiftsgate is synonymous with the Himalayan climbing rose known to the world as *Rosa filipes* 'Kiftsgate', a vigorous plant that is allowed to grow at will and flowers profusely in June. This is just one of a huge range of roses and other plants that grow in the informal terraced gardens that run down the hill below the house, offering fine views over the Vale of Evesham.

Kiftsgate Court

South of Chipping Campden is the village of ★ **Broad Campden**, where C.R. Ashbee *(see page 49)* lived in a delightful house converted from a ruined Norman chapel. The house is all but invisible behind its high yew hedge topped by topiary birds, but the village is delightfully grouped around a green with a tiny house-sized church.

Continuing south you will skirt Northwick Park, with its splendid house of 1686 (now converted to apartments) before entering the attractive village of ★★ **Blockley**. This village is built on a series of terraces above the deep valley of the Knee Brook. From the village you can look across to the open pasture on the opposite hill, grazed by sheep today, as it was in medieval times when the bishops of Worcester cleared the village of Upton, moving its inhabitants in order to create more grazing for their vast flocks. Bumps in the pasture show quite clearly where the old houses used to stand.

Blockley was where the sheep were brought to be sheared before their wool was washed, spun and woven in the mills at the bottom of the valley. When overseas competition destroyed the local wool-processing industry, local entrepreneurs converted their mills to the production of silk. As a result, several that still survive (now converted to private houses) have names like the Old Silk Mill or the Ribbon Mill. Wandering the maze of paths through the village, past brightly coloured front gardens, you will spot the former weavers' cottages by their attic windows; the grander houses belonged to the mill owners. The perfect way to see Blockley is when the gardens are open under the National Gardens Scheme (usually on the weekend closest to Midsummer Day). If you don't happen to be around at that time, you can at least visit ★ **Mill Dene Garden** (tel: 01386 700457; open Apr–Oct, Mon–Fri 10am–6pm) with its beautiful stream garden planted around the water course that feeds the mill pool. From the top of the garden there are extensive views, with the church as a backdrop.

South of Blockley there are several more fine gardens to visit and the order in which you visit them will depend on the day of the week and the time of day. Batsford opens at 10am most days, whereas Bourton House and Sezincote have more restrictive hours.

★★ **Sezincote** is the most spectacular, and it is worth planning your trip to fit it in (no telephone; garden open Thur, Fri and Bank Holiday Mon 2–6pm every month except Dec; house open May, Jun, Jul and Sept, Thur and Fri 2.30–6pm,). Sezincote is an exotic delight that ought not to fit into the Cotswold countryside but does so supremely well. Inspired by northern Indian temples and fortresses, it combines homely Cotswold features with chattris and chajas, peacock-tail windows and colonnades, statues of Brahmin bulls and a reproduction of Hyder Ali Khan's mausoleum. Put together, the result is a building so astonishing that the Prince Regent, visiting in 1807, told his architect to scrap all existing plans for the Brighton Pavilion, and 'build me something like Sezincote'. Those who tour the house will discover that the oriental elements are all on the outside – inside it is a

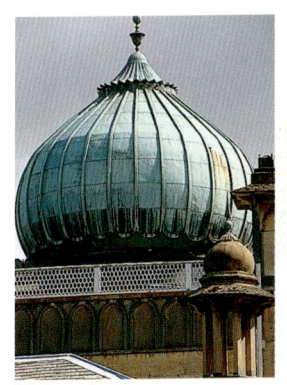

Glorious Sezincote

more conventional Regency house – but the building served its purpose in reminding the client, Sir Charles Cockerell, of his beloved India, where he had served for many years with the East India Company.

The gardens (among the finest in Gloucestershire) are built around a natural stream that bubbles out of the ground on the hill above before being channelled by a series of pools and cascades through temples and between banks brimming with moisture-loving plants. Clumps of bamboo, delicate Japanese maples, weeping birches and beeches all thrive in these conditions, adding interest and continuing the oriental theme.

Sezincote is not the only garden in the vicinity inspired by memories of the Orient. At ★★ **Batsford Park**, reached through Bourton-on-the-Hill, the arboretum was planted from 1886 by Lord Redesdale, who had been on diplomatic service in Tokyo. When he returned he planted his garden with the flowering cherries, magnolias and maples that are such a feature of Japanese landscapes (tel: 01386 701441; open Mar–mid Nov, daily 10am–5pm; rest of year Sat and Sun 10am–4pm). Spring and autumn are the best times to visit for outstanding colour, but the magnificent vistas and the garden centre make this a place worth visiting throughout the season. Also located here is the ★ **Cotswold Falconry Centre** (tel: 01386 701043; open mid-Feb–mid-Nov, daily 10.30am–5.30pm) where you can watch birds of prey in the aviaries through closed-circuit television, and view demonstrations as eagles, hawks, owls and falcons show off their hunting skills.

Back in **Bourton-on-the-Hill**, a fine village whose charms are difficult to appreciate fully because of heavy traffic, ★★ **Bourton House** is a more conventional 3-acre (1.2-hectare) English garden set around a handsome manor house with topiary, knot gardens and flamboyant borders stuffed full of unusual plants, some of which are for sale (tel: 01386 700121; open end May–end Oct, Thur and Fri 10am–5pm).

★ **Moreton-in-Marsh**, a good place for refreshment, is full of handsome former coaching inns, such as the Manor House Hotel of 1658, the White Hart of 1782 and the 18th-century Redesdale Arms. These grand old watering-holes all cater for visitors who come to shop, especially on Tuesday, when a huge market fills the long and broad main street. Buildings of note in the town include the Curfew Tower, opposite the Market Hall. It was built in the 16th century and used to ring the curfew every night until 1860, warning householders to cover their fires, a necessary precaution in the days when timber buildings regularly burned to the ground in the night because of stray sparks.

Pretty as a picture in Bourton-on-the-Hill

Redesdale coat of arms

Route 7

Stow's Old Stocks Hotel

Around Stow-on-the-Wold

Stow-on-the-Wold – Abbotswood – Lower Slaughter – Upper Slaughter – Naunton – Guiting Power – Temple Guiting – Bourton-on-the-Water – Northleach – Chedworth *See map page 42*

★★ **Stow-on-the-Wold**, according to an ancient rhyme, is 'where the wind blows cold'. The truth of this becomes chillingly apparent if you visit Stow, the Cotswolds' highest town (situated at around 754 ft/230 metres) on a grey day in February, but in summer the town has a festive atmosphere, packed with coach trippers or antique hunters coming to browse in the town's numerous good art and antique galleries *(see Shopping, page 72)*.

Stow's huge market square testifies to the size of the flocks that used to be driven here for sale between 1107 (when Henry I granted the town its charter) and the 1980s, when the Stow Horse Fairs were finally moved away from the town because of the crime and chaos they created. Wooden stocks survive on the green in Stow's market place as a warning to miscreants.

Stow's ★★ **church** contains memorials to several of those who died in the last (and perhaps the fiercest) battle of the Civil War, which took place on 21 March 1646. The church was used as a prison and held some 1,000 plus Royalists at one time, suffering much damage as a result. The curious north porch, which has two yew trees flanking the doorway growing out of the masonry, was added as part of the 1680 restoration, while inside there is a fine slate floor memorial near the altar to the Royalist, Hastings Keyt, dressed in uniform sash and helmet. Easily missed at the back of the church is a naturalistically

Stow's church

carved hare, part of a Saxon carving from the first church on the site, founded in AD 986.

Surrounding Stow are some of the Cotswolds' prettiest villages. One mile (1.6 km) west, ★ **Lower Swell** (the name perhaps refers to the ancient well in the village) has some remarkable Norman carvings in its generally over-restored church, and a village war memorial designed by Edwin Lutyens, who was also the architect of nearby Abbotswood house – see it if you can when the excellent gardens are open under the National Gardens Scheme.

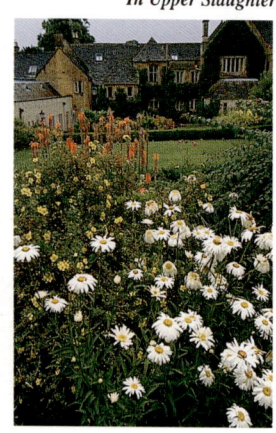

★★ **Lower Slaughter**, 2 miles (3 km) south, is almost too perfect, and the slough (or marsh) from which the village derives its name has been tidied up, so that the River Eye now flows between grassy banks and colourful cottage gardens beneath a series of simple stone bridges. At the western end of the village you can visit the mill (tel: 01451 820052; open daily 10am–6pm), last used commercially in 1958. An ambitious restoration programme began in 2002,but the bottle shop and tea rooms (famous for home-made ice-cream) remain open.

A delightful lane follows the Eye upstream to ★★★ **Upper Slaughter**, with a good view on the right of the Elizabethan manor (now a hotel, *see page 79*) as you enter the village. The church has many fine Norman details, but its most curious feature is the large, mock-medieval tomb of the Reverend F. E. Witts (died 1854), whose *Diary of a Cotswold Parson* was discovered and published some years ago. For a short but interesting walk through the village, take the left-hand path from the church and turn left to reach the point where the Eye forms a ford. Turn right by the ford and walk up the trout-filled stream, past banks of bullrushes and waterside plants where dragonflies dart. Turn right uphill once the path meets the road to return to the village green in front of the church.

The road to ★ **Naunton**, 4 miles (6 km) west, passes through a valley filled with the kinds of flowers that only grow on unimproved limestone pasture – cowslips in spring, yellow rattle and rare orchids in summer. The village church has an interesting monument to Ambrose Oldys, vicar of Adderbury in Oxfordshire, who was 'barbarously murthered by ye rebells' in 1645. The inscription tells of his unshakeable loyalty to the Crown and his adherence to the established Church. The lovely dovecot in the village has recently been restored by volunteers.

★ **Guiting Power** is another handsome village, with a fine 15th-century cross carved with the Virgin and Child and the Crucifixion standing on the green. The fine cruciform church has an hourglass carved in stone over the doorway to remind us of the brevity of life and there are a variety of humorous portrait heads carved on the roof

Lower Slaughter

In Upper Slaughter

supports inside. ★ **Temple Guiting** (so called because it once belonged to the Knights Templar) is not as pretty, but its church does have a fine 18th-century nave and an intricately modelled plaster coat of arms of George II, flanked by a rampant lion and unicorn.

At Cotswold Farm Park

To the east, reached via Kineton, is the ★★★ **Cotswold Farm Park** (tel: 01451 850307; open mid-Mar–mid-Sept, daily 10.30am–4pm). Founded by Joe Henson in 1970, this was the first farm in England to specialise in the rescue of rare breeds of farm animal, and it is the headquarters of the Rare Breeds Survival Trust. Some of the animals here were only just rescued from extinction: the White Park Cattle, for example, an ancient Celtic (pre-Roman) strain once bred for hunting and for ornament, and the Norfolk Horn Sheep (down to the last four rams and five ewes before a breeding programme was initiated). To young visitors, the real appeal is that they are nearly all friendly, contented and placid animals. There is also an adventure playground and a touch barn to explore, full of lambs, calves, rabbits and baby goats.

Another cluster of children's attractions can be found in ★★★ **Bourton-on-the-Water**, 6 miles (10 km) south. This whole village is given over to tourism, but even the tacky gift shops do not detract from the charm of what has been dubbed 'the Venice of the Cotswolds' because of the elegant 18th-century bridges that cross the River Windrush as it flows through the centre of the village. One of Bourton's best attractions is the enchanting ★★ **Model Village** (tel: 01451 820467; open daily 9am–6pm in summer; 10am–4pm in winter) depicting Bourton (as it was in 1937) at one-ninth scale. Keep an eye out for novel features such as the bonsai trees, or the choir and organ music just discernible if you put your ear to the door of the parish church. Close by is ★★ **Birdland** (tel: 01451 820480; open Apr–Oct, daily 10am–6pm; rest of year to 4pm). The best time to visit is at around 2.30pm when the 500 or so birds are fed, from the fruit-eating parrots to the fish-eating penguins. Most of the birds here were bred at the park and they are so tame that they are allowed to wander freely.

Bourton's Model Village

Birdland parrot

Bourton's other attractions include the ★ **Bourton Model Railway** (tel: 01451 820686; open Apr–Sept, daily 11am–5.30pm; rest of year weekends only; closed Jan), which will entertain anyone with nostalgic yearnings for the train set of their youth, the ★ **Cotswold Perfumery** (tel: 01451 820698; open Mon–Sat 9.30am–5pm; Sun 10am–5pm), with exhibits and a programme on how perfumes are made, and the ★★ **Cotswold Motoring Museum and Toy Collection** (tel: 01451 821255; open Feb–Nov, daily 10am–6pm). The latter is the home of Brum, which younger children will recognise as the little yellow car that features in the TV programme of the same name. The museum is also an Aladdin's cave of motoring memorabilia. The road signs, vintage caravans and advertisements are all immediate reminders of the nearly forgotten but not-too-distant past.

If the idea of Bourton's crowds is not for you, children might be satisfied with a visit to ★★ **Folly Farm**, on the western outskirts of the village, off the A436 (tel: 01451 820940; open daily 10am–5pm). The farm is home to a huge collection of wild and domestic fowl – ducks, geese and chickens in all their colourful variety, and there is a well stocked garden centre and shop alongside.

From Bourton, you can either take the direct road to Northleach along the A429 Fosse Way, or you can meander through three of the least-spoiled villages to be found in the Cotswolds: Notgrove, Turkdean and Hampnett. The idyllic setting of ★ **Notgrove**'s church alone makes it worth a visit, but other treasures include a tapestry made in 1954 showing the village, church and manor glimpsed through hazel trees (a reference to the village name), and a lovely stained-glass fragment of around 1300, depicting the Virgin and Child. ★ **Turkdean**'s church is an archaeological puzzle, a patchwork of Norman masonry, the remains of a 15th-century St Christopher wall painting and stained glass put up in 1924. ★★ **Hampnett** looks as if time stopped here some time in the pre-industrial age, with its farmhouses grouped around a rough green where the River Leach springs out of the ground and begins its journey to join the Thames at Lechlade. The church, with its Norman carvings of birds on the chancel-arch capitals, is made more delightful by the 19th-century wall paintings, executed by the rector, the Reverend Wiggin, in an attempt to recreate the original Norman appearance.

Hampnett village

The road from Hampnett joins the A429 just above the former prison at **Northleach**, now converted to form a museum of rural life called the ★★ **Cotswold Heritage Centre** (tel: 01451 860715; open Apr–Oct, Mon–Sat 10.30am–5pm, Sun noon–5pm). Built in 1791, the prison reflected the reforming ideas of local philanthropist, Sir George Onesiphorus Paul, and it set new standards for prison health and hygiene. The cell block and courthouse survive, with informative displays on the prison regime. The rest of the building is devoted to exhibits illustrating farming life through the seasons and the work of a Victorian kitchen and dairy.

Cotswold Heritage Centre

By contrast, ★★ **Keith Harding's World of Mechanical Music**, in the town centre, is concerned with the intricate niceties of antique musical boxes and clocks, self-playing pianos and early gramophones (tel: 01451 860181; open daily 10am–6pm). Guided tours include demonstrations of the exhibits. From the museum it is a short step up the churchyard path to one of the Cotswolds' finest chuches, built with profits from the wool trade. Evidence of the industry is found throughout the ★★ **church**; the printed guide will tell you where to find fine 15th-century brasses decorated with sheep, woolsacks, woolmarks and shears. Some have dates in Arabic numerals, indicating trade contact with Spain and North Africa. Best of all is the Fortey brass, with its border decorated with slugs, snails, hedgehogs and strawberries.

A little light music

South of Northleach, signs will direct you to the remains of ★★ **Chedworth Roman Villa**, delightfully set in a wooded combe overlooking the Coln Valley (tel: 01242 890256; open Apr–Oct, Tue–Sun and bank holidays 10am–5pm; Mar, and first half of Nov, Tues–Sun 11am–4pm). The mosaics here include a charming depiction of the seasons, with winter personified as a peasant in a billowing hooded cloak, bringing home a hare for the pot and a branch for fuel. In one corner of the site is a nymphaeum, a small sanctuary to the goddess of the spring that supplied the villa and its bathhouse with water. The Roman inhabitants introduced the edible snails that are found in and around the villa, especially on damp days, and which inhabit the railway cuttings above the villa, now a nature reserve.

Hands on in Chedworth Roman Villa

★ **Chedworth church** is another handsome Norman building, and its stone-carved 15th-century pulpit is one of the finest in the Cotswolds. Not far away is the atmospheric Seven Tuns pub, with its outdoor terrace and excellent food – the perfect place to relax and contemplate the delightful way in which the pretty houses of Chedworth seem to cling to a series of terraces above the steep Coln Valley.

The villa's museum

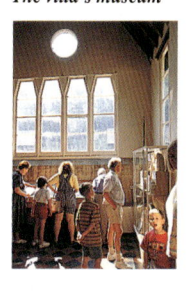

Route 8

The Coln and Windrush Valleys

Ampney Crucis – Ampney St Mary – Ampney St Peter – Quenington – Coln St Aldwyns – Hatherop – Fairford – Lechlade – Kelmscott – Southrop – Eastleach Turville and Martin – Burford – the Barringtons – Sherborne – Bibury – Coln Rogers – Coln St Dennis – Barnsley *See map page 42*

Many of the brooks, streams and rivers that rise in the high Cotswolds are tributaries of the Thames. Nearly all of them meet in a network of silvery threads in and around the town of Lechlade, where the dip slope of the Cotswold limestone meets the gravels of the Thames Valley. Springs and a plentiful supply of fresh water meant that these valleys have been settled since the earliest times.

Most villages on this route have late Saxon churches, such as the fine church at ★ **Ampney Crucis**, 3 miles (5 km) east of Cirencester. Gone are the 14th-century wall paintings, but a copy of one hung still hangs in the tower, showing the particularly gruesome martyrdom of St Erasmus. The main highlight is the flamboyant tomb of George Lloyd (died 1584) with its pedimented canopy, looking like a miniature temple.

Tomb of George Lloyd

A short way down the A417 the church at ★ **Ampney St Mary** stands alone in fields beside the Ampney Brook. The original village was abandoned in 1348, when it was struck by plague, and a new village was created a mile (1.6 km) to the northeast. An intriguing Norman sculpture on the north wall depicts the triumph of good, in the form of a lion, over evil, a two-headed serpent. The 14th-century wall paintings within depict St Christopher, St George and the Dragon and a Christ of the Trades, a symbolic mural representing the wounds inflicted on Christ by those who work on the Sabbath.

Also Saxon, though considerably enlarged in the 19th century, is the delightfully situated church at ★ **Ampney St Peter**. Restorers spared the licentious carving on the west wall of the nave, though by that time the genitals had probably already been hacked off!

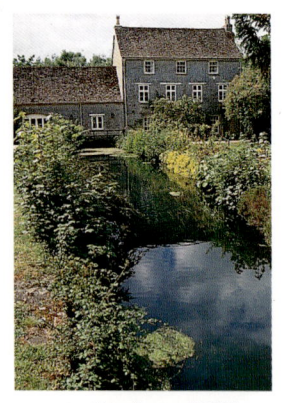

Quenington Mill House

A long, straight road leads to ★★ **Quenington**, where the church and the mill (now a private house, but the gardens are occasionally open under the National Gardens Scheme) form a fine group with the 13th-century gateway to Quenington Court, once a Commandery of the Knights Hospitaller. Much of the interest at Quenington lies in the Romanesque carvings round the north and south doorways, so do not worry if the church is locked. The south door has a vigorous carving of the Harrowing of Hell; Christ appears thrusting a spear into the mouth of a figure representing hell, while praying figures rise from the dead. The opposite door shows the Coronation of the Virgin, with Christ seated in Majesty surrounded by symbols of the Evangelists, and a beautiful domed building that represents the new Jerusalem, or the Temple of Heaven. Beakheads, a rare Romanesque feature, surround the arch; amongst the usual dragons and monsters are more familiar creatures, including a horse, a hare and a badger.

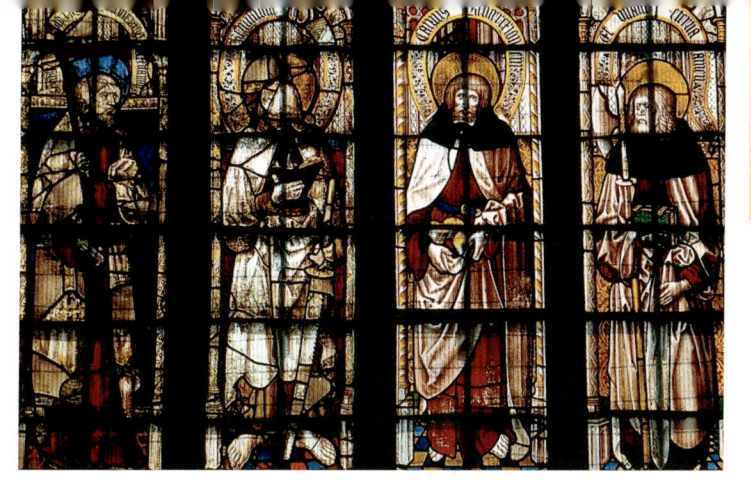

Upstream lies ★ **Coln St Aldwyns**, an estate village that benefited greatly from the funds poured into it by the local squire, Sir Michael Hicks-Beach (1837–1916), a former Chancellor of the Exchequer. Hicks-Beach's house was substantially reduced in size after the war, and some of the timber and stone was used to build the fine pedimented row of estate cottages opposite the church. It is the doorway of the church that again commands attention, with its bold and deeply undercut chevron mouldings and two fine dragonhead stops.

At neighbouring ★ **Hatherop**, Lord de Mauley's French Gothic house is now a school. The church in the grounds (built in the 1850s) is remarkable for the mortuary chapel of Barbara, Lady de Mauley (died 1844), depicted in a lovingly sculpted monument by Raffaelle Monti, with praying angels at her head and feet. The chapel itself is carved with a stone frieze in which wildflowers, butterflies and the letter B for Barbara are intertwined.

★★★ **Fairford**, 3 miles (5 km) due south of Hatherop, glories in perhaps the finest of all the Cotswold wool churches, built at the expense of the local wool merchants, John and Edmund Tame. Of primary interest is the almost complete sequence of 15th-century stained glass made in the workshops of Barnard Flower, master

Fairford stained glass

Quenington carving

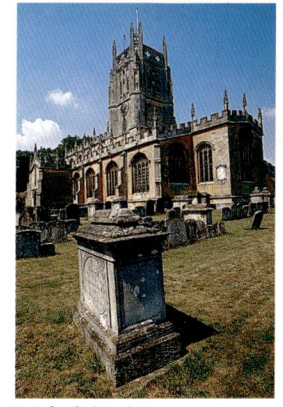

Fairford church

glass painter to Henry VII and the man who created the glass for Westminster Abbey's Lady Chapel. The whole Biblical story, from the Creation to the Crucifixion, is depicted here, though it is the Last Judgement window, with its fiery red devils, that holds the most interest (bring binoculars to enjoy the grim details of diabolical punishment and torture). Of great importance, too, is the woodwork of the chancel screen (dating from between 1501–1527, and featuring carved pomegranates, the emblem of Catherine of Aragon, wife first of Prince Arthur and then of Arthur's younger brother, Henry VIII) and the misericords depicting scenes from popular fables, such as the story of Reynard the Fox. Among several fine tombs in the churchyard, look for the grave of Tiddles, the church cat.

★★ **Lechlade**, 5 miles (8 km) east, has a church that inspired Shelley to write the sonnet, 'A Summer Evening Churchyard' in 1815. Lechlade marked the end of a holiday in which the poet had rowed up the Thames from Windsor. The footpath he took from the river to the town is now an attractive tree-lined path called, inevitably, Shelley's Walk. It is worth following in his footsteps across the fields to St John's Bridge for a fine backwards view of Lechlade's graceful church spire rising above the water meadows. St John's Bridge marks the highest navigable point along the river, and the bridge itself, though 19th century, stands on one of the earliest stone bridges to be built across the Thames. Beside the nearby lock is a stone statue of Neptune, carved by the same Rafaelle Monti responsible for the Hatherop effigy.

By the bridge is the excellent (though often crowded) Trout Inn. The minor road alongside heads through flat fields to the pretty village of ★★ **Kelmscott**, where the **manor** is famous as the summer residence of William Morris between 1871 and 1896 (tel: 01367 252486; open Apr–Sept, Wed 11am–1pm and 2–5pm; additionally on 3rd Sat in Apr, May, Jun and Sept, and the 1st and 3rd Sat in Jul and Aug 2–5pm). The barn beside the manor contains a comprehensive account of Morris and his time at Kelmscott. Several buildings in the village exemplify the arts and crafts tradition that Morris founded, including the Morris Cottages (built by Jane Morris as a memorial to her husband in 1902), with a relief of Morris carved in stone on the facade, and the village hall, designed by Ernest Gimson. Jane and William Morris share a grave beneath a simple stone tomb in the rustic village churchyard, designed to resemble a Viking tomb-house.

Heading northwards again, we reach the valley of the River Leach at ★ **Southrop**, where the church is a must for its unusual Norman font, carved with armoured figures rep-

St John's Bridge

Kelmscott Manor

Morris relief

resenting the Virtues trampling on beasts that represent the Vices. The names of the Virtues are carved in the arches above, while the names of the Vices are written in mirror writing below, as if to emphasise the polarity or opposition of each Vice to its corresponding Virtue.

Many fine houses, surrounded by beautifully laid stone walls and threaded by the gentle river, make this village one of the most attractive in the area, though there is strong competition from ★ **Eastleach Turville** and ★ **Eastleach Martin**, to the north. Here the two parish churches stand almost next to each other on opposite banks of the river, linked by an ancient stone clapper bridge.

Two more popular visitor attractions are to be found along the A361 Lechlade to Burford Road. The pretty village of Filkins is home to the ★ **Cotswold Woollen Weavers**, an enterprise that has revived the crafts of spinning and weaving by hand and using traditional machinery (tel: 01367 860491; open Mon–Sat 10am–6pm, Sun 2–6pm). Three miles (5 km) north is the ★★ **Cotswold Wildlife Park**, the perfect place to spend a day with children, with its narrow-gauge railway, children's farmyard, reptile houses and aquarium, not to mention the incongruous sight of zebras, rhinos and tigers roaming in Cotswold paddocks in front of a Gothic-style manor house (tel: 01993 823006; open daily 10am–6pm).

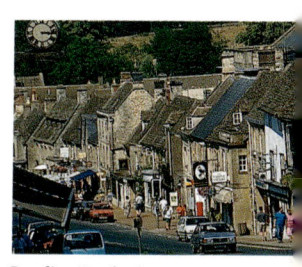

At Cotswold Woollen Weavers

★★ **Burford**, 4 miles (6 km) to the north, is often described as over-commercialised, but its charms shouldn't be ignored. It has one of the Cotswolds' finest high streets, lined with attractive 17th- and 18th-century houses, descending steeply to a packhorse bridge over the River Windrush. The massive cathedral-like church stands by the river. In the 19th century the church was so badly treated by restorers that an outraged William Morris was provoked into forming the Society for the Protection of Ancient Buildings (SPAB). However, there is much left to enjoy, including the splendid Renaissance monument to Edward Harman (died 1569), barber and surgeon to Henry VIII, which is decorated with Red Indians. East of Burford, off the A40, is ★★ **Minster Lovell**, an exceptionally attractive village with a fine Perpendicular church and the ruined 15th-century **Minster Lovell Hall** (open during daylight hours).

Bustling Burford

Packhorse bridge at Burford

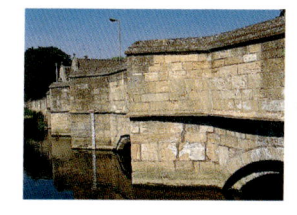

West of Burford, the Windrush flows through a series of unspoiled villages. Quarries at Taynton and the Barringtons supplied stone for such notable buildings as Windsor Castle, Blenheim Palace, the crypt of St Paul's Cathedral, several post-Fire of London churches and several Oxford colleges. They also supplied the skilled masons to work the stone, one of whom built the back lane that runs from ★ **Great Barrington** downhill to the

A summer's day in Sherborne

Time to quench your thirst?

Sherborne's watermeadows

Bibury inn

millstream, over the Windrush and up to the church at ★ **Little Barrington**. Known as Strong's Causeway, the lane was built under the terms of the will of Thomas Strong, a local man whom Sir Christopher Wren appointed as his chief mason for the rebuilding of St Paul's Cathedral.

In Great Barrington church, several monuments testify to the sculptors' skills, including those to the Bray children (died 1720) by Christopher Cass, and to Mary Countess Talbot (died 1787) by Joseph Nollekens. By contrast, Little Barrington's church is a simple Norman building with carvings of Christ in Majesty.

If you follow Strong's Causeway down to the river, you will note how wild and natural the Windrush looks for much of its course. Several local landowners are committed to wildlife conservation, resulting in a corridor of undrained watermeadow 15 miles (24 km) in length.

At ★★ **Sherborne** (National Trust), the 18th-century watermeadows are being restored, including the sluice gates and channels that flood the fields in winter to protect grass from frost damage and thus produce early grazing (for a leaflet with suggested walks, contact the Sherborne Estate Office, tel: 01451 844257). Sherborne village was built as a model estate village in the mid-19th century, and it consists of distinctive rows of identical stone cottages. The main house (now apartments) has a magnificently flamboyant facade (1663). The church alongside contains a cluster of good monuments, including one that features a fashionably décolletage angel carved by Richard Westmacott in 1791. Also here is **Lodge Park**, a unique example of a 17th-century hunting lodge, beautifully restored by the National Trust (tel: 01684 855369; open March to end Oct, Fri–Mon, 11am–4pm).

Climbing out of the Windrush valley, cross the bare tops southwards to rejoin the Coln valley at ★★ **Bibury**, which

William Morris called the prettiest village in England (Henry Ford agreed; in the 1920s he tried to buy houses in the village to transport back to America). The River Coln flows along the main village street, beside a green expanse of boggy watermeadow known as Rack Isle. To one side are the picturesque Arlington Row cottages, built in 1380 as a monastic wool store. In the 17th century, this was converted into a row of weavers' cottages, and the cloth produced here was sent to Arlington Mill, on the other side of Rack Isle, for fulling (degreasing). Once the cloth had been thoroughly pounded and washed at the mill, it was hung to dry on timber frames on Rack Isle.

Today **Arlington Mill** is open to visitors and contains informative displays on the history and workings of the mill (tel: 01285 740368; open daily 10am–6pm). The next-door **Trout Farm** lets you learn how a trout fishery works, and you can fish for your supper (tel: 01285 740215; open daily 9am–6pm, 10am–6pm on Sun; 9am–5pm in winter). Quieter attractions await at the other end of the village, where the unusually large **church** stands alongside Bibury Court, built in 1633 (now a hotel, *see page 79*). Some of the original Saxon church survives, including fragments of cross shaft carved with interlace. There is a fine stained-glass window in the chancel by Karl Parsons (1884–1934).

As you approach ★ **Barnsley**, to the south, you will first skirt the tree-filled grounds of Barnsley Park, which is not normally open to the public (except during the annual Barnsley Festival in early May), before entering the main street of this showcase village, where until quite recently telephone wires, overhead cables and TV aerials were banned as a way of preserving its timeless appearance.

The village is famous for ★★ **Barnsley House**, where the 4-acre (1.6-hectare) garden has had a massive influence on its many visitors, including Prince Charles (tel: 01285 740561; open Mon, Wed, Thur and Sat 10am–5.30pm; closed Christmas to end Jan). The creator of the garden, Rosemary Very, died in 2001, and the house was put on the market in 2002. It is likely that any new owner will keep the garden open but check before making a visit by contacting the Cirencester Tourist Information Centre (tel: 01285-654 180). The framework of the garden was created in the 1960s by the late David Verey, who rescued various stone structures from demolished buildings in the area and used them to create gazebos and focal points for beds and borders. He has a simple memorial in the garden, inscribed with words by John Evelyn, that sum up the love of gardening: 'As no man be very miserable that is master of a garden here; so no man will ever be happy who is not sure of a Garden hereafter… where the first Adam fell, the second rose.'

Arlington Row

At the trout farm

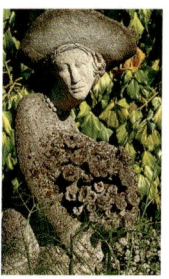

At Barnsley House

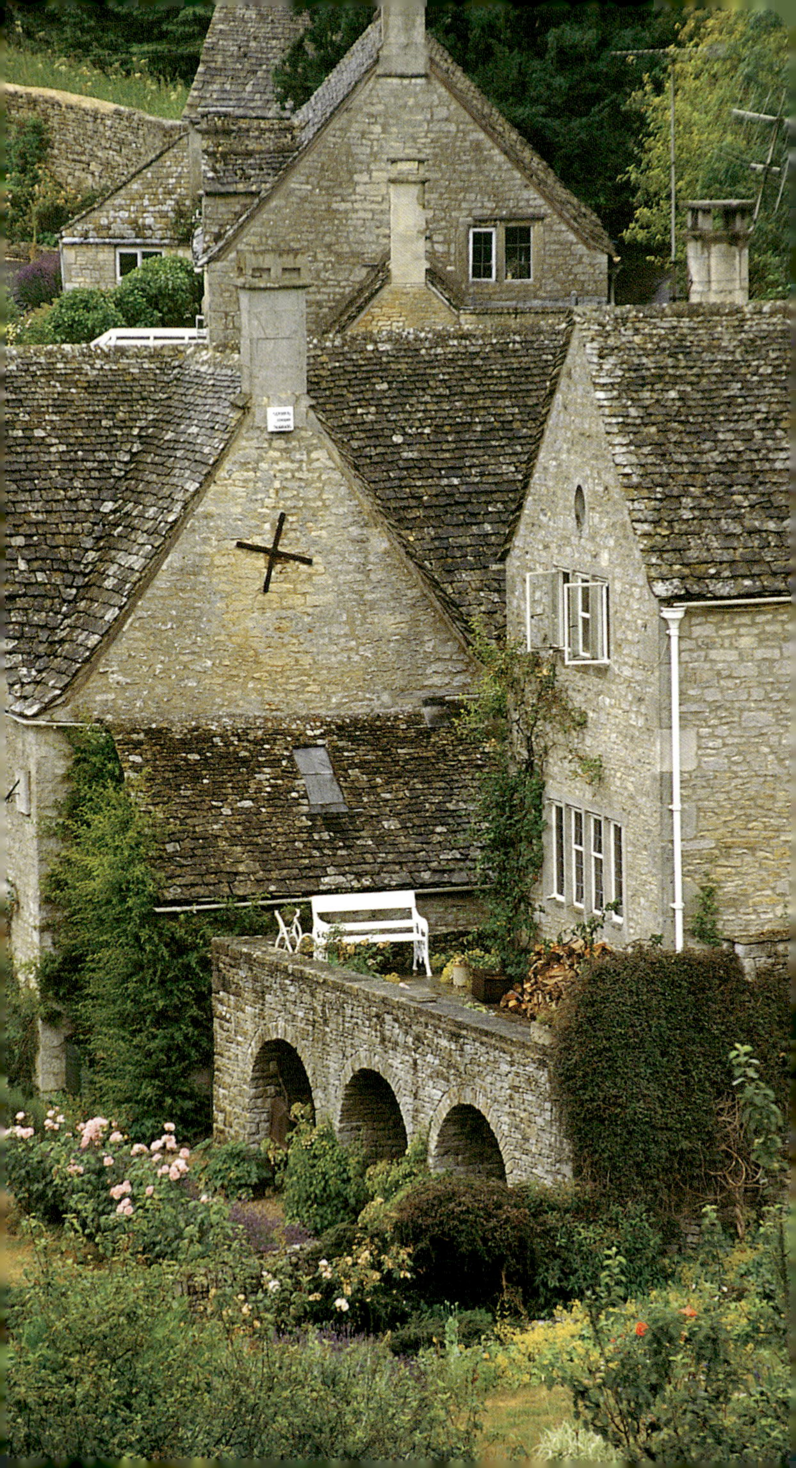

Architecture and Gardens

Architecture

The Cotswolds' architectural style is simple yet effective. Roofs are very steeply pitched – they have to be to carry the weight of the stone tiles. The tiles are applied in a fish-scale pattern, starting with the smallest, hand-sized tiles at the ridges and descending to table-sized tiles at the eaves. The eaves overhang the walls because, in the absence of guttering, this was the best way of carrying rainwater well away from the walls. Other features that look decorative but which are entirely practical do the same job of shedding water, especially the drip moulds found around the chimney stack and above windows and doors.

Window frames are also made of stone, usually with a cross-shaped mullion (upright bar) and transom (horizontal bar) dividing the space into four, with two tall lights in the bottom half and two smaller lights above.

These are the basic ingredients of almost all Cotswold architecture. Some buildings have extra features – dormer windows or Italianate details such as round or lozenge-shaped windows or rusticated quoins and door and window surrounds – but by and large this simple style was used on every type of building, from barns and churches to cottages and manors. A grand Elizabethan building like Bibury Court is essentially a larger version of the Arlington Row weavers' cottages in the same village.

The principal difference between the houses of the rich and the poor is that grander buildings were constructed of cut-stone (known as ashlar), with mortar joints so narrow as to be almost invisible. Humbler buildings were made of rubble – stones of random size – cemented by thick beds of lime mortar. Rubble buildings were frequently limewashed to give them the same smooth appearance as their grander neighbours (the bare stone that characterises towns and villages today is a comparatively recent phenomenon). The effect of adding colours to the limewash resulted in a polychromatic look that had its own charm. An example of this style can be seen in Cirencester Market Place, where the buildings are painted in shades of yellow, red, blue and green, and in Great Badminton village, where the buildings are still limewashed in traditional ochre and bull's blood.

Cotswold churches have some unusual Romanesque features. Elkstone church is the outstanding example: it has a corbel table (projecting stones running round the chancel exterior at eaves level, carved with animals, birds and symbols of the zodiac), a tympanum (a semicircular slab of stone above the doorway) carved with a Biblical scene (in this case Christ in Majesty with the Evangelists) and an arch around the tympanum carved with

Opposite: quintessential Cotswolds architecture, Bisley

Tiled roof

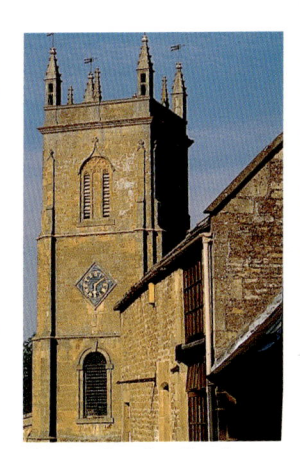

Chipping Campden Church

beakheads (monsters, birds and animals with beak-shaped snouts that bite the roll moulding). Inside, the chancel arch is enriched with bold moulding called zig-zag or chevron moulding, and the arch moulding ends in stops carved in the shape of dragon heads.

Scholars have plotted the distribution of these features and come up with various explanations for their origin. Some, like the dragon heads, are probably motifs that survive from pagan Anglo-Saxon wood carving. Other features, like the corbels, tympanum and beakheads, came to the Cotswolds from France and Spain by way of the Compostella pilgrimage route. Medieval pilgrims came back full of enthusiasm for the Romanesque churches they had seen along the route, and asked local Cotswold masons to produce something similar. In some cases, the details have become charmingly domestic, as at Quenington, where the beast heads include a horse and a badger.

Canals brought new materials, such as brick, to the Cotswolds in the late 18th century and building styles began to change – Cheltenham, for example, looks very different from most other Cotswold towns because it was largely constructed by speculative builders using pattern books based on what was in vogue in London at the time.

The arts-and-crafts movement, however, brought a reaction against this eclecticism, and those towns and villages where the movement was at its most active have some very fine 20th-century buildings that look as if they have been there for centuries. There were several different arts-and-crafts groups espousing the ethics of William Morris, fleeing from London like the great artist to seek a refuge from urban ugliness and industrial values. Following in Morris's stead were C.R. Ashbee, who moved from the Mile End Road to set up the Guild of Handicrafts (a craft-based community) in Chipping Campden in 1902, and the Cotswold arts-and-crafts movement, led by Ernest Gimson and the Barnsley brothers, Ernest and Sydney, set up at about the same time. The legacy of these architects, designers and craftsmen can be seen in churches (stained glass and furnishings), in museums (Cheltenham) and in stately homes in the region (Owlpen Manor, for example).

Allied to the arts-and-crafts movement was the Cotswold 'school' of gardening, whose leading lights included Charles Wade at Snowshill Manor, Mark Fenwick at Abbotswood and Lawrence Johnston at Hidcote. They owe their architectural style (with garden rooms defined by yew hedges and steps, pools and gazebos forming important focal components) to the influence of Edwardian architects such as Sir Edwin Lutyens and Oliver Hill. More recent gardens, such as Barnsley House, also spring from this tradition, for although the planting is pastel and gentle, there are formal elements.

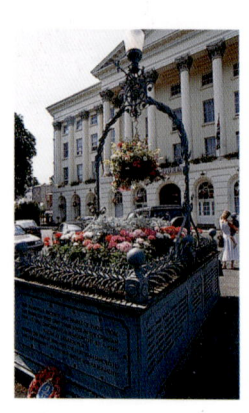

Regency-style Cheltenham

Owlpen Manor

Festivals

Folklore festivals

Many folkloric events take place in the Cotswolds, providing lots of family fun (tourist information centres will supply precise dates which vary from year to year). The **Cooper's Hill cheese rolling contest** *(see page 38)* takes place on Whit Monday (children can also scramble for the sweets that are traditionally scattered to ensure a good and plentiful harvest). On the same Bank Holiday weekend in Tetbury, the **Woolsack Races** *(see page 22)* close the town centre, while the people of Chipping Campden enjoy their **Cotswold Olympicks** *(see page 49)*.

On or around 16 May, the wells at **Bisley** are decorated with flowers and blessed. Cotswold churches often look at their best for the harvest festivals that take place in September. Painswick celebrates its ancient **Clipping Ceremony** on or around 19 September, when children from the parish, wearing wreaths of flowers in their hair, link hands to form a circle right round the church (clipping derives from *clyppan*, meaning to embrace) while singing songs to the accompaniment of the town band. Many Cotswold towns still have a **Mop Fair** in the autumn. These are relics of the hiring fairs of old when labourers and domestic servants wore symbols of their trade in order to attract the attention of potential employers. **Cirencester**'s fair is one of the best (held on the first two Mondays in October, or on the first three if Monday falls on the 11th).

Cultural festivals

The Cotswolds calendar is crowded with events of both national and local significance. There are local choral, organ and small ensemble concerts in parish churches throughout the Cotswolds – look at church noticeboards to see what's on. At the national end of the scale there are the two Cheltenham Festivals: the **Cheltenham Festival of Music** (many of whose concerts are broadcast live on Radio 3) takes place in July and the **Daily Telegraph Cheltenham Festival of Literature**, a talking shop for authors and poets, takes place in October (tel: 01242 227979 to make bookings for both festivals, or log on to www.cheltenhamfestivals.co.uk for more details). Of the many local festivals that take place over the year, the **Stroud Festival**, held in early September, is perhaps the best, with an eclectic range of theatrical events, folk and classical concerts (tel: 01453 760900; www.stroudfestival.co.uk).

The popular summer exhibition of **Gloucestershire Guild Crafts** takes place in Painswick from the end of July to the end of August, and is just one of several showcases for the best of local art (tel: 01452 814745).

Festive fun

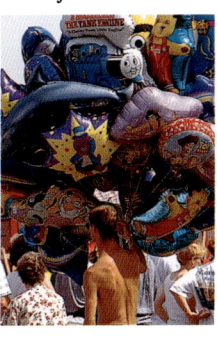

Spring-time revels in Lechlade

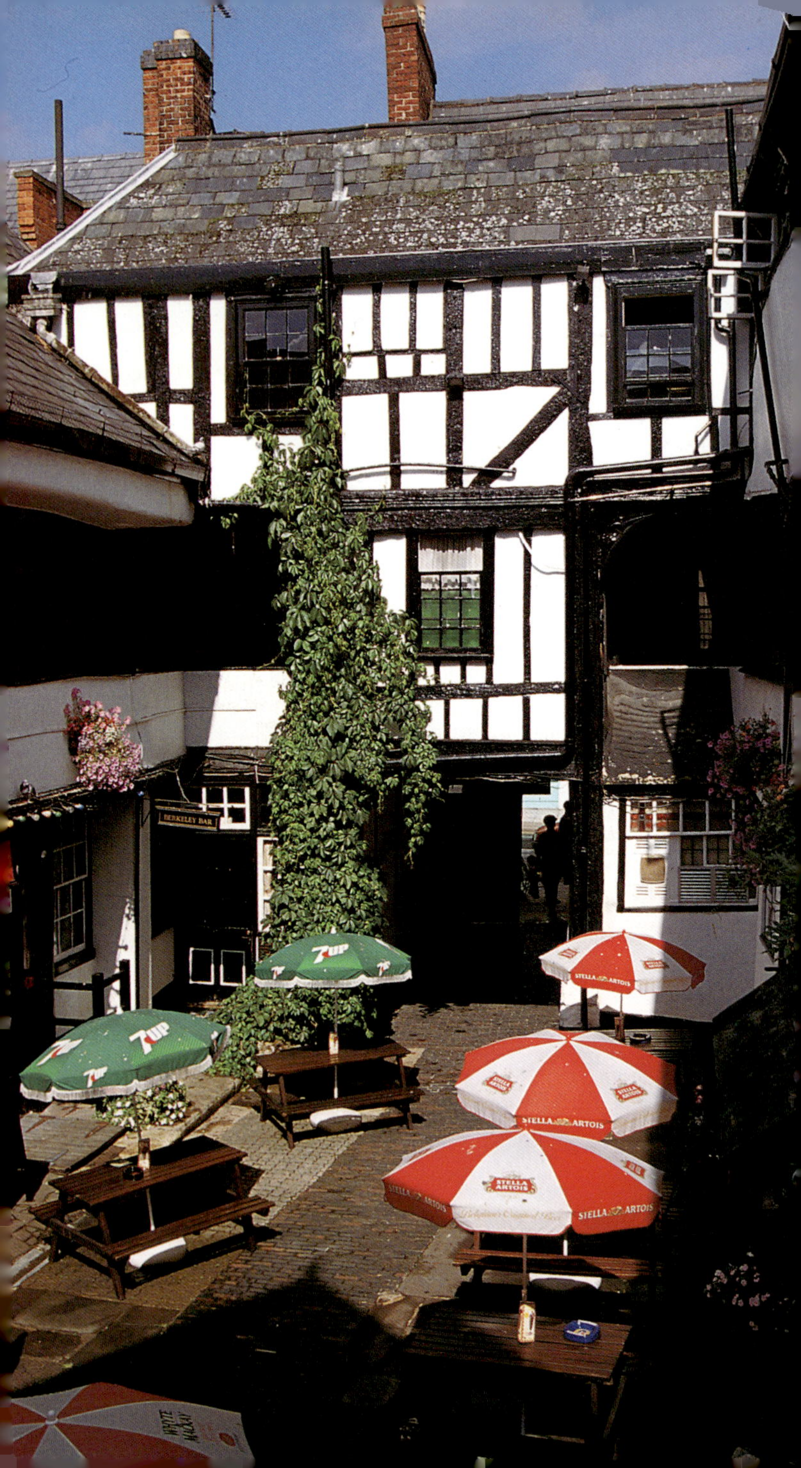
BERKELEY BAR
7UP
STELLA ARTOIS

Food and Drink

Opposite: New Inn Gloucester

The Cotswolds is very affluent and there are plenty of expensive restaurants in the region happy to part customers from their money in return for rather second-rate food and service. There are few truly outstanding restaurants in the region, but just about every village and town in the Cotswolds has a welcoming pub serving tasty and unpretentious food at perfectly reasonable prices.

The Cotswolds has no regional specialities, but you may be fortunate and come across pubs or restaurants serving organically produced meat – Gloucester Old Spot pork is undergoing a popular revival, and Prince Charles's Highgrove estate is just one local source of organic beef, lamb and pork. You may also find excellent dairy products, from home-made ice creams to local cheeses such as Single and Double Gloucester and North Cerney goat's cheese.

Shop for local produce

Restaurants

£££ (over £65 for two)
££ (£40-65 for two)
£ (under £40 for two)
Price guides include house wine.

Kelmscott hostelry

South Cotswolds

£ Bathurst Arms, North Cerney. Tel: 01285 831281. Set beside the pretty River Churn, with an extensive garden used in summer for occasional barbecues. Try warm goat's cheese salad made with cheese produced at the nearby North Cerney House *(see page 40)*, mixed grill, pasta dishes or panfried fish.

£ The Bear, Bisley. Tel: 01452 770265. Unspoiled traditional pub in a very attractive village. Serves a good range of bar snacks, such as French sticks filled with steak, bacon and sausage or bacon and melted cheese or vegetarian pasties, plus a good choice of garlic-enhanced meat, fish and pasta dishes.

£ Black Horse, Cranham. Tel: 01452 812217. Come in summer and you may well find a folk evening in full swing or Morris men dancing for a well-earned pint. This cosy pub serves good, freshly made food, including a range of popular meat and vegetarian pies, pheasant in season, nut loaf, sausages and fishcake. Children welcome.

Try the local brew

£ Brewery Arts, Brewery Court, Cirencester. Tel: 01285 657181. An ideal lunch venue set in the Brewery arts complex in Cirencester, serving homemade wholefood, vegetarian dishes and cakes, plus filling soups with homebaked bread, all at very reasonable prices.

£ The Café, 1 Brewery Court, Cirencester. Tel: 01285 658686. Lunch on Italian-influenced sandwiches, salads or soups, with a choice of breads featuring sun-dried

Calcot Manor

Daneway Inn's garden

A pub lunch in Broadway

tomatoes or olives. Giant stuffed brie or salt-beef sandwiches are a complete meal in themselves.

£–££ Calcot Manor, Tetbury. Tel: 01666 890391. Choose between the bar meals in the friendly and unpretentious Gumstool Inn, or the romantic candle-lit restaurant. The menu changes regularly according to the season, but perennial offerings range from traditional sirloin steak, roast duck and charcoal-grilled sole to Mediterranean-influenced pasta dishes and salads. **£** in bar, **££** in restaurant.

£ Crown of Crucis, Ampney Crucis, Cirencester. Tel: 01285 851806. Reliably good food at reasonable prices including a special children's menu. Try homemade sausages, a ploughman's or the excellent vegetarian pancakes for lunch or order the more substantial balti dishes and pies for dinner.

£ Daneway Inn, Sapperton. Tel: 01285 760297. This popular pub is located in the Golden Valley, just below Sapperton, set beside the now derelict Thames and Severn Canal. During its long history, this pub has served the 18th-century navvies who built the canal and the leggers who propelled boats through the long canal tunnel that begins a short distance up the valley. Today it is popular with walkers exploring the towpath who come to stoke up on ploughman's lunches, baked potatoes, lasagne or beef and Guinness pie.

££ Mad Hatters, 3 Cossack Square, Nailsworth. Tel: 01453 832615. Nailsworth has become something of a gastronomic centre, with its festival of food in September and its several good food shops and restaurants. Mad Hatters is a wholly organic restaurant renowned for its excellent Sunday lunches (bookings must be made by noon the previous day) as well as competent cuisine and art-lined walls.

££ The New Inn, Coln St Aldwyns. Tel; 01285 750651.

Villagers fought against plans to close this old coaching inn some years ago, and it has since been turned into a great place to eat, with inexpensive but fresh and inventive bar snacks, or more substantial dishes (which attract rave reviews from food critics) in the garden or candle-lit restaurant (for which bookings are advised).

££ **Trouble House**, Tetbury. Tel: 01666 504508. Recently taken over by Michael Bedford (formerly head chef at City Rhodes) and his wife, the Trouble House has been transformed into a relaxed gastro-pub serving top-quality food at pub prices. Do be sure to book.

££ **White Horse**, Frampton Mansell. Tel: 01285 760960. Another first-rate gastro pub between Cirencester and Stroud, run with flair by Shaun and Emma Davis – you can view the menus at www.members.aol.com/whitehorse11/whitehorse.htm

££ **Village Pub**, Barnsley. Tel: 01285 740421. An upmarket Gastropub decorated in country house style, and serving the kind of food rarely found outside London – Pacific Rim flavours using top-quality local organic ingredients.

North Cotswolds

£ **Black Horse**, Naunton. Tel: 01451 850565. Comfortable pub full of old wooden furniture where you can choose from bar snacks such as a ploughman's or half a pint of prawns, or go for the restaurant offerings of pasta, salmon fishcakes, steaks, gammon or local lamb chops.

£ **Crown Inn**, High Street, Blockley. Tel: 01386 700245. French cuisine in the brasserie, or daily specials in the bar, with an emphasis on seafood and fresh fish. Popular dishes include cod deep fried in a batter made with chives and beer, mussels and seafood *vol-au-vent*.

£££ **Lygon Arms**, High Street, Broadway. Tel: 01386 840318. The cost of lunch or dinner at this renowned Michelin-starred restaurant can easily soar into the stratosphere unless you stick to the fixed-price menu, but committed foodies will not begrudge the cost. Attention to every detail ensures that even straightforward sounding dishes are transformed into a gourmet experience – including the three-course vegetarian menu.

£££ **Old Wool House**, Market Place, Northleach. Tel: 01451 860366. Authentic French cuisine in the heart of the Cotswolds, with excellent game (in particular hare and venison) a speciality in season, plus fresh fish and hearty meat dishes. Dinner only. Closed Sun and Mon. Set menu.

£ **Red Lion**, Chipping Campden High Street. Tel: 01386 840760. At the opposite end of the High Street from the church, this popular old beamed coaching inn, with its numerous quiet niches, welcomes children and serves everything from a full meat and two veg lunch to bar snacks, including the excellent pork and leek sausages which come with crusty French bread.

The esteemed Lygon Arms

Keeping cool in Bourton

Shopping

Cheltenham is the place to shop if you want maximum choice and leading stores: here you can pick from the upmarket couturiers that line the Promenade, the delights of Cavendish House (a miniature Harrods with its Food Hall and departments selling everything from clothes to household furnishings), the delicatessens lining Regent Street and the antique and craft shops of Montpellier. The High Street has HMV, Virgin, Marks & Spencer, Boots and the Disney Shop, and there are two huge arcades – the Beechwood Shopping Centre and the Regent Arcade, on the opposite side of the High Street (the Regent arcade has Kit Williams' delightful clock featuring a giant bubble-blowing goldfish).

Several towns are outstanding for antiques: Tetbury is almost one big antique shop, selling everything from museum-quality clocks and furniture to cheap collectables. Tetbury also has two good food shops: the House of Cheese (13 Market Place) and Tetbury Traditional Meats (31 Church Street), which sells sausages, dry-cured bacon and organic meat from Prince Charles's Highgrove estate.

Stow-on-the Wold is another antiques centre. Do not miss Christopher Clarke, in Sheep Street, whose stock ranges from Renaissance bronzes to English landscapes. Also in Stow is Scotts of Stow, the kitchenware mail order company, which has one retail outlet in the Square and another selling cheap discontinued lines in Park Street. Almost opposite the Park Street shop is the Brewery Yard selling oriental rugs, and the boutique of Jenny Edwards-Moss, whose handmade clothes are exquisitely tailored.

Cirencester's own Brewery Yard is one of the best places to shop for arts and crafts in southern England. There are permanent workshops selling everything from brightly patterned waistcoats and children's clothes to wicker baskets and hand-thrown pottery. Changing exhibitions focus on the work of local sculptors, painters and textile designers, and the shop is crammed with inexpensive crafts, from jewellery to toys and mobiles.

Markets offer a chance for foodies to sample good local produce. The Tuesday market at Moreton-in-Marsh is the biggest in the area, while Cirencester has markets on Monday and Friday. If you miss them, head for Jeroboams, the well-stocked food and wine shop on Cirencester Market Place, just west of the church, for Italian and French breads, continental salamis, cheeses, salads and grilled Mediterranean vegetables. Jesse Smith's, in nearby Black Jack Street, has won many awards for its sausages, raised pies and meat from rare breeds and organic farms. This old shop draws as many visitors for its Edwardian tiled decor as for the quality of its stock.

Open-air art, Cheltenham

Tetbury is good for antiques

Active Pursuits

Cycling: Cycle hire companies are located at Moreton-in-Marsh railway station (Country Lanes Cycle Centre, tel: 01608 650065), in Chipping Campden (Cotswold Country Cycles, tel: 01386 438 706) and Bourton-on-the-Water (Hartwells Cycle Hire, tel: 01451 820405).

Game fishing: The Lechlade Trout Fishery offers half-day, full-day and evening tickets for fly fishing on the River Leach and on two lakes. For more details, call the Fishery; tel: 01367 253266.

Golf: The following clubs, all set in scenic escarpment-edge locations, can accommodate day visitors: Cotswold Edge (Wotton-under-Edge), tel: 01453 844167; Minchinhampton Common, tel: 01453 832642; Minchinhampton New Club, tel: 01453 833866; Painswick, tel: 01452 812180; Stinchcombe Hill, tel: 01453 543878.

Jet skiing: Jet Ski UK is based at the Cotswold Water Park, a series of flooded gravel workings between South Cerney and Ashton Keynes. Equipment for hire and tuition. Tel: 01285 861345.

Riding: Off-road horse riding and tuition for all ages and abilities at Woodlands (based near Winchcombe), tel: 01386 584404, or at the Camp Riding Centre (based near Stroud), tel: 01285 821219.

Sailing, surfboarding and watersports: Lots of opportunities exist in the Cotswold Water Park, which has blossomed into a major leisure resort, offering every kind of watersport. For further details, tel: 01285 861459, or visit the new Water Park Office and Information Centre at Spratsgate Lane, Shorncote, near Cirencester.

Swimming, squash, badminton: The Cotswold Leisure Centre, off the A419 on the Cirencester ring road, has a 25-metre pool, a children's pool and courts. In addition, there is a fitness centre, solarium and a sauna for those seeking land-based activities. Tel: 01285 654057.

Walking: Long-distance footpaths include the Gloucestershire Way, the Cotswold Way, the MacMillan Way and the Monarch Way. The Cotswold ANOB Partnership (tel: 01451 226554; email: tourism@cheltenham-gov.uk) organises an excellent programme of guided walks throughout the year. If you are planning to walk the Cotswold Way, Compass Holidays (tel: 01242 250642) offers an accommodation booking and luggage transfer service.

Freewheeling

Only for the brave

Ready to ride

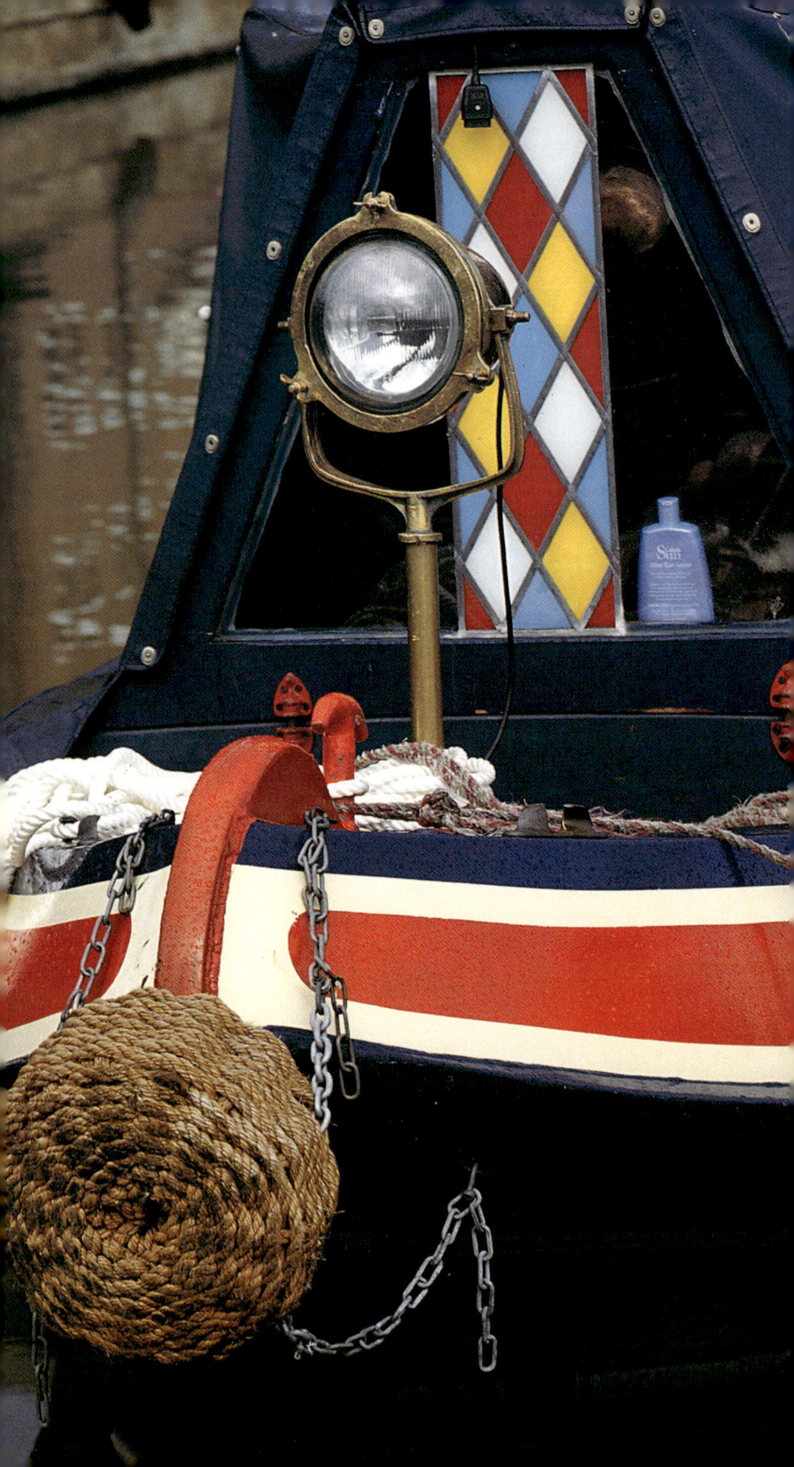

Getting There

By car
From London, the M4 and M40 motorways provide access to the Cotswolds within three hours. The M4 also provides rapid access from Wales, Somerset, Devon and Cornwall, and the M5 from the Midlands and the north.

By coach
National Express operates daily services from all parts of the UK to Cheltenham, calling at Cirencester, Stow-on-the-Wold, Northleach and Gloucester. For bookings and information, tel: 08705 808080, or visit the company's website at www.nationalexpress.co.uk

By rail
Brunel's Great Western Railway is one of the most scenic lines in southern England, especially the 'Golden Valley' line from Swindon to Cheltenham via Kemble, Stroud, Stonehouse and Gloucester. A line also runs from Paddington to Worcester via Oxford and Moreton-in-Marsh (journey time to Moreton-in-Marsh, 1 hour 40 minutes). South West and West Railway runs services to Cheltenham and Gloucester from Wales, the Midlands and southwest England. For further information, call the National Rail Enquiry Service (24-hour advance timetable and fare information on 0845 748 4950, or visit their website at www.railtrack.co.uk You can buy tickets online at www.thetrainline.com

By air
The nearest international airport is Bristol. For airport information, tel: 01275 474444, or see Ceefax, page 452.

Getting Around

Public transport
With determination, you can get around the Cotswolds using public transport, but expect to use taxis to reach destinations not on bus or train routes. Tourist information centres can supply timetables, or you can also write for a copy of the Public Transport County Map for Gloucestershire by contacting the Public Transport Team, Environment Department, Shire Hall, Gloucester, Glos GL1 2TH, tel: 01452 425543.

Taxis
Bourton-on-the-Water, David Prout, tel: 01451 821478
Cheltenham, Central Taxis, tel: 01242 228877
Cirencester, Radio Cars, tel: 01285 650850
Tetbury, Martin's Car, tel: 01666 503611.

Opposite: narrowboat in Gloucester docks

Most people come by car

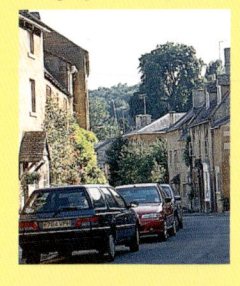

Another approach

Hop on a bus

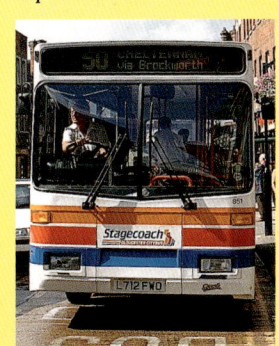

A great way to explore

Out and about in Gloucester

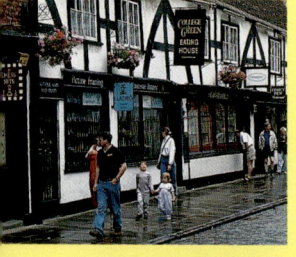

Call for help

Facts for the Visitor

Tourist information
Bourton-on-the-Water, Victoria Street, Bourton-on-the-Water, Glos, GL54 2BU, tel: 01451 820211
Burford, The Brewery, Sheep Street, Burford, Oxon OX18 4 LP, tel: 01993 823558.
Cheltenham, 77 Promenade, Cheltenham, Glos GL50 1PP, tel: 01242 522878.
Cirencester, Market Place, Cirencester, Glos GL7 2NW, tel: 01285 654180.
Gloucester, St Michael's Tower, The Cross, Gloucester, tel: 01452 421188.
Moreton-in-Marsh, Cotswold District Council Offices, High Street, Glos GL56 0AZ, tel: 01608 650881.
Stow-on-the-Wold, Hollis House, The Square, Glos GL54 1AF, tel: 01451 831082.
Stroud, Subscription Room, George Street, Glos, GL5 1AE, tel: 01453 765768.
Websites: Tourist Information for the Cotswold District: www.cotswold.gov.uk/tourism; Stroud area: www.thisisstroud.com; for Gloucestershire: www.visit-glos.org.uk and www.cotswoldguides.org.uk

Guided tours
Cotswold and Gloucestershire Tourist Guides, tel: 01242 226554. These are qualified Green Badge Guides, with extensive knowledge and a real enthusiasm for the region. Many have specialist interests, so tours can be tailored to suit individual requirements. Several European languages are spoken – telephone for details.
Compass Holidays, tel: 01242 250642, specialises in services for walkers including personalized walking tours, accommodation pre-booking and luggage transfer.

Emergencies
In emergency dial 999 for all services.
AA Breakdown, tel: 0800 887766
RAC breakdown, tel: 0800 828282

Hospitals
Cheltenham General, Sandford Road, tel: 01242 222222.
Cirencester Hospital, Tetbury Road, tel: 01285 655711.
Gloucestershire Royal, Great Western Road, Gloucester, tel: 01452 394600 (emergency unit).
Stroud General, Trinity Road, tel: 01453 562200.

Police stations
In an emergency, dial 999. For non-emergency calls, dial one of the two central switchboard numbers – 01452 521201 or 01242 521321 – and your call will be directed to the nearest or most appropriate police station.

The Cotswolds for Children

There are several destinations in the Cotswolds which will keep children and adults alike amused all day.

For younger children, the Bourton-on-the-Water area has the excellent **Cotswold Farm Park**(*see page 55*), which has an adventure playground and touch barn, in addition to the animals themselves, which are friendly and enjoy being fed. Take a picnic if the weather is fine. If you want to see more wildlife, you could go on to **Birdland** *(see page 55)*, in Bourton, or to **Folly Farm** *(see page 56)*, just to the north, for exotic birds or waterfowl.

Continuing with the animal theme, the **Cotswold Wildlife Park** near Burford *(see page 61)* is a complete day's outing. As well as a wide variety of animals, it is an excellent place for a family meal, offering sensibly priced chips, chicken, burgers and fish fingers, even if service is a little slow at peak times.

Slimbridge *(see page 15)* is best treated as a half-day's outing and could be combined with **Berkeley Castle** *(see page 14)*, where children's taste for the gruesome will be stimulated by the cell where Edward II was imprisoned and the grim dungeon alongside. The Cotswolds' other important castle, at **Sudeley** *(see page 45)*, scores high marks for its big adventure playground, but many of the exhibits will probably be too grown-up for young children's tastes.

Among the museums on offer in the region, those at **Cirencester** *(see page 34)* and **Northleach** *(see page 57)* are excellent for older children, while the **Cheltenham Art Gallery and Museum** *(see page 43)*, the **Gloucester Folk Museum** *(see page 19)* and the **Gloucester City Museum** *(see page 21)* all have excellent displays and quiz sheets or hands-on activities aimed at children who can read and write fairly well.

Chedworth Roman Villa *(see page 57)* also has special archaeological weekends aimed at inquisitive children, often on Bank Holiday weekends. Best of all, though, is the **National Waterways Museum** in Gloucester *(see page 18)*, which offers a range of computer-based activities and quiz sheets plus boats to explore and an activity room where trained assistants are on hand to help children with painting or modelling on most summer weekends. If you have time, a visit here should ideally be combined with a **boat-trip** on the Gloucester and Sharpness Canal.

For simply running about and rolling in the grass, or hunting for fossils and insects, **Crickley Hill** is a good destination *(see page 38)*. It has an informative visitor's centre with clear and concise explanations of the local archaeology and wildlife.

Cotswold Farm Park

Adding to the atmosphere, Berkeley Castle

At the National Waterways Museum

Accommodation

Broadway Hotel

An option in Tetbury

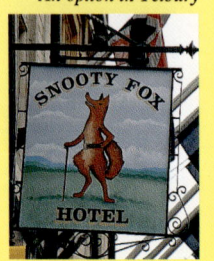

Staying in the Cotswolds, you can live like an aristocrat and stay in a fine country house hotel or you can hire a Romany caravan and play at being a gypsy for a week. There are plenty of bed and breakfast establishments, and several camping and caravanning sites, as well as youth hostels and cottages to rent. For full information, write to the Cotswold Visitor Information Centre, Hollis House, Stow-on-the-Wold, Glos GL54 1AF, and ask for their free accommodation guides. Tourist Information Centres (*see page 76*) will also book accommodation.

Self catering

The **National Trust** owns hundreds of acres of scenic Cotswold farmland, and it has converted some of its estate cottages into self-catering accommodation. Choose between a thatched cottage for two or an elegant farmhouse sleeping up to 10, in the picture-book village of Snowshill. Alternatively, you could go for a lock-keeper's cottage at Buscot sleeping four. Details from National Trust Enterprises, PO Box 536, Melksham, Wiltshire SN12 8SX, tel: 0870 458 4422, www.nationaltrustcottages.co.uk

Even more unusual accommodation can be let from the **Landmark Trust**, which specialises in restoring historic buildings and letting them out. In the Cotswolds, the Trust owns the East Banqueting House, a Jacobean baroque building in Chipping Campden (sleeps six), and Field House in Minchinhampton, an 18th-century stone house, sleeping seven. Details from the Landmark Trust, Shottesbrooke, Maidenhead, Berkshire SL6 3SW, tel: 01628 825925, fax: 01628 825417; www.landmarktrust.co.uk

Another wonderful hideaway is **Owlpen**, near Uley, where the Tudor manor house *(see page 26)*, restored in 1926 by Norman Jewson, is surrounded by lovely cottages and mill buildings that have been converted to self-catering accommodation. For details contact Bookings, Owlpen Manor, Owlpen, near Uley, Glos GL11 5BZ, tel: 01453 860261; www.owlpen.com

Hotels and guesthouses

£ (£50–80 per night double)
££ (£80–120 a night double)
£££ (over £120 a night)

North Cotswolds
£ Andrews Hotel, 99 High Street, Burford OX18 4QA. Tel: 01993 823151. Fax: 01993 823240. Good value accommmodation in an area more generally noted for high prices. The hotel is set in a mellow Tudor building full of beams and maze-like corridors. Peaceful and relaxing.

£ Cleeve Hill Hotel, Cleeve Hill, Cheltenham, Glos GL52 3PR. Tel: 01242 672052, Fax: 01242 679969. Smart guesthouse in an Edwardian building with views over Cleeve Hill.

£ Crown Inn, High Street, Blockley, Moreton-in-Marsh GL56 9EX. Tel: 01386 700245. Fax: 700247. This friendly hotel has the atmosphere of an old coaching inn. Good French cuisine in the brasserie, or daily specials in the bar.

£££ Lords of the Manor Hotel, Upper Slaughter, Glos GL54 2JD. Tel: 01451 820243. Fax: 01451 820696. A much extended 17th-century rectory set in idyllic parkland, with the River Eye meandering through the grounds.

Lords of the Manor Hotel

£££ Lower Slaughter Manor, Lower Slaughter, Glos GL54 2HP. Tel: 01451 820456. Fax: 01451 822150. This 17th-century manor, on the edge of one of the Cotswolds' prettiest villages, offers tennis courts, a croquet lawn and putting green, an indoor pool and sauna.

Lower Slaughter Manor

£££ The Lygon Arms, Broadway, Worcestershire WR12 7DU. Tel: 01386 852255. Fax: 01386 858611. Spoil yourself in one of England's finest hotels, a magnificent 16th-century coaching inn, renowned as much for its restaurant as for its antique furnishings and roaring log fires.

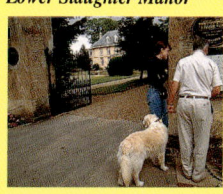

South Cotswolds

££ Bibury Court, Bibury, Glos GL7 5NT. Tel: 01285 740337. Fax: 01285 740660. This glorious Jacobean house fulfils everyone's idea of the perfect Cotswold manor. Rarely does such a sense of history come with such a low price tag. Two people can enjoy a room for around £80.

££ Calcot Manor, Tetbury, Glos GL8 8YJ. Tel: 01666 890391. Fax: 01666 890394. Calcot Manor, with its 17th-century farm buildings, has been converted into a complex combining one of the area's most popular restaurants, the Gumstool Inn, and a separate hotel with a range of rooms: choose between four-posters and antiques, or family rooms with children's bunk beds and a play room.

£ Crown of Crucis, Ampney Crucis, Cirencester Glos GL7 5RS. Tel: 01285 851806. Fax: 01285 851735. A 16th-century inn in a peaceful setting overlooking the village cricket pitch and the Ampney Brook. Good food.

££ Old Bell Hotel, Abbey Row, Malmesbury SN16 0AG. Tel: 01666 822344. Fax: 01666 825145. Betjeman sang the praises of this wisteria-clad hotel. Log fires and comfortable antique furniture, but far from stuffy (children are welcome). Good value, with double rooms at around £80.

£££ Swan Hotel, Bibury, Glos GL7 5NW. Tel: 01285 740695. Fax: 01285 740473. Elegant creeper-clad hotel on the banks of the River Coln. Sumptuous rooms and bathrooms, beautiful gardens and fishing rights.

Swan Hotel, Bibury

£ Tavern House, Willesley, Tetbury, Glos GL8 8QU. Tel: 01666 880444. Fax: 01666 880254. Upmarket B&B in former coaching inn near Westonbirt Arboretum.

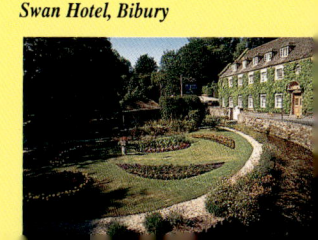

Index

Accommodation......78–9
Aderley......................25
Amberley....................29
Ampney Crucis............58
Ampney St Mary.........58
Ampney St Peter.........58
architecture.........9, 65–7
Arlingham..................17
Arlington Mill.............63
arts-and-crafts
  movements.........49, 66
Avening......................30

Badminton Park..........24
Bagendon..................40
Barnsley.....................63
Batsford Park..............52
Baunton.....................40
Berkeley.....................14
Berkeley Castle...........14
Beverston...................27
Bibury..................62, 65
Birdlip Country Park...38
Bisley...................31, 67
Blockley.....................51
Bourton House...........52
Bourton-on-the-Hill....52
Bourton-on-the-Water.....
  55–6
Broad Campden..........50
Broadway...................47
Broadway Country
  Park........................47
Burford.................61–2

Cerney House
  Gardens..................40
Chalford....................30
Chavenage House.......27
Chedworth Roman
  Villa........................57
cheese rolling contest,
  Cooper's Hill......38, 67
Cheltenham......41–4, 66,
  67, 72
  Art Gallery and
    Museum...............43
  Holst Birthplace
    Museum...............43
  Museum of Costume 44
  Promenade.............43
  racecourse..............44
Cherington.................30
Chipping Campden .48–9
Cirencester....7, 34–5, 65
  Agricultural College...7
  Corinium Museum....34
  parish church..........34
Cleeve Hill.............5, 44
clothmaking..........7, 28

Coberley.....................39
Coln St Aldwyns.........59
conservation............8–9
Cooper's Hill..............38
Cotswold Falconry
  Centre....................52
Cotswold Farm Park....55
Cotswold Olympics..11,
  49
Cotswold Water
  Park........................73
Cotswold Way..............5
Cotswold Wildlife
  Park........................61
Cotswold Woollen
  Mill........................61
Cotswold Woollen
  Weavers..................61
Cowley......................39
Cowley Manor...........39
Cranham...................37
Crickley Hill Country
  Park........................38

Daglingworth.............35
Daneway Banks.........31
Didmarton................23
Doughton Manor.......23
Dover's Hill...............49
Duntisbourne Abbots
  church....................36
Duntisbourne Leer.....35
Duntisbourne Rouse...35

Eastleach Martin........61
Eastleach Turville......61
economy.....................7
Elkstone...............39, 65

Fairford.....................59
Folly Farm.................56
Frampton Manor........17
Frampton Mansell......30
Frampton on Severn...17
Frocester...................33

Gatcombe Park......8, 29
Gloucester............18–21
  Cathedral............20–1
  City Museum and Art
    Gallery.................21
  Folk Museum.........19
  Gloucester Gaol......19
  Museum of
    Advertising...........18
  National Waterways
    Museum...............18
  Queen Boadicea II...18
  Soldiers of Gloucester-
    shire Museum.......19

Tailor of Gloucester
  Museum.................20
Gloucester–Warwick-
  shire Railway..........45
Great Badminton...24, 65
Great Barrington........62
Great Witcombe Roman
  Villa........................37
Guiting Power...........54

Hailes Abbey............45
Hampnett..................56
Hardwicke Court........17
Haresfield.................32
Haresfield Beacon......32
Hatherop..................59
Hawkesbury..............24
Hetty Pegler's Tump...26
Hidcote Manor
  Gardens..................50
Highgrove...........11, 23
Horton......................24

Jenner Museum.........14
Jet Age Museum........21

Kelmscott................60
Kiftsgate...................50
King's Stanley...........33

Lechlade...................60
Little Barrington........62
Leckhampton Country
  Park........................38
Lee, Laurie............5, 31
Leonard Stanley.........32
Little Badminton........24
Little Sodbury hillfort .24
Lower Slaughter.........54
Lower Swell..............54

Minchinhampton.......29
Minster Lovell...........80
Misarden Park Gardens
  and Nursery............36
Miserden..................36
Moreton-in-Marsh......52
Morris, William....33, 60,
  66

Nailsworth...............29
Naunton....................54
Newark.....................25
Nibley Knoll..............25
North Cerney............40
Northleach................57
Notgrove..................56

Owlpen....................26
Owlpen Manor....26, 66

Ozleworth..................25

Painswick..............31-2
Painswick Beacon......32
Painswick Rococo
  Garden...................32
Prinknash Abbey........37
Prinknash Pottery.......37

Quenington...............58

Rare Breeds Survival
  Trust.................11, 55
Rendcomb.................40
restaurants............69–71

St Augustine's Farm...17
Sapperton..................31
Selsley......................33
Seven Springs............38
Severn Bore..............17
Sezincote..................51
Sharpness..................15
Sherborne..................62
shopping...................72
Slad Valley............5, 31
Slimbridge...........11, 15
Snowshill Manor...47, 66
Southrop................60–1
sports.......................73
Standish....................32
Stanton.....................46
Stanway....................46
Stow-on-the-Wold...53–4
Stroud......................28
Sudeley Castle...........45

Temple Guiting.........54
Tetbury.....................22
  Police Bygones
    Museum...............22
Turkdean..................56
Tyndale Monument.....25

Uley.........................26
Uley Bury Iron Age
  hillfort....................26
Upper Slaughter.........54

Watledge.................29
Westonbirt................23
Wildfowl and Wetlands
  Trust, Slimbridge......15
Whiteway.................36
Winchcombe.............45
Woodchester Unfinished
  Mansion.................27
woolsack races,
  Tetbury....................6
Wotton-under-Edge.....25